Business Result

SECOND EDITION

Starter *Teacher's Book*

John Hughes

Great Clarendon Street, Oxford, OX2 6DP, United Kingdom

Oxford University Press is a department of the University of Oxford. It furthers the University's objective of excellence in research, scholarship, and education by publishing worldwide. Oxford is a registered trade mark of Oxford University Press in the UK and in certain other countries

First published in 2018

2022 2021 2020 2019 2018

10 9 8 7 6 5 4 3 2 1

ISBN: 978 0 19 473862 0   Book
ISBN: 978 0 19 473861 3   Pack

Printed in China

This book is printed on paper from certified and well-managed sources

ACKNOWLEDGEMENTS

Cover image: Getty Images/Mikael Dubois

Back cover photograph: Oxford University Press building/David Fisher

Contents

Introduction

The course

Who is *Business Result Second Edition* for?

Business Result Second Edition is a comprehensive multi-level course in business English suitable for a wide range of learners. The main emphasis is on *enabling* your students, helping them to communicate more effectively in their working lives.

In-work students

Unlike many business English courses, *Business Result Second Edition* addresses the language and communication needs of employees at all levels of an organization, who need to use English at work. It recognizes that the business world is truly international, and that many people working in a modern, global environment spend much of their time doing everyday tasks in English – communicating with colleagues and work contacts by phone, via email and in a range of face-to-face situations, such as formal and informal meetings/discussions, and various planned and unplanned social encounters. It contains topics and activities that allow the students to participate in a way that is relevant to them, whatever their level in their company or organization.

Pre-work learners

Business Result Second Edition can also be used with pre-work learners at college level. The course covers a variety of engaging topics over the 8 units, so students without much work experience will receive a wide-ranging overview of the business world, as well as acquiring the key communication skills they will need in their future working lives. Each unit in this *Teacher's Book* contains suggestions for adapting the material to the needs of these students.

One-to-one teaching

Many of the activities in the book are designed for use with groups of students, but they can also be easily adapted to suit a one-to-one teaching situation. Notes in the individual *Teacher's Book* units offer suggestions and help with this.

What approach does *Business Result Second Edition* take?

Business Result Second Edition helps students communicate in English in real-life work situations. The priority at all times is on enabling them to do so more effectively and with confidence. The target language in each unit has been carefully selected to ensure that students will be equipped with genuinely useful, transferable language that they can take out of the classroom and use immediately in the workplace.

The course recognizes that, with so many businesses now being staffed by people of different nationalities, there is an increasing trend towards using English as the language of internal communication in many organizations. As well as learning appropriate language for communicating externally – with clients or suppliers, for example – students are also given the opportunity to practise in situations that take place within an organization, such as giving a report, making arrangements and taking part in meetings.

The main emphasis of the course is on the students speaking and trying out the target language in meaningful and authentic ways; it is expected that a large proportion of the lesson time will be spent on activating students' interest and encouraging them to talk. The material intentionally takes a communicative, heads-up approach, maximizing the amount of classroom time available to focus on and practise the target language. However, you will also find that there is plenty of support in terms of reference notes, written practice and review material.

The syllabus is essentially communication-driven. The topics in each of the 8 units have been chosen because of their relevance to modern business and the world of work. Vocabulary is presented in realistic contexts with reference to real companies or organizations. Grammar is also a key element of each unit. It is presented in an authentic context and ensures that students pay attention to accuracy, as well as become more proficient at expressing themselves clearly and precisely. The *Business communication* sections ensure that students are provided with a range of key expressions they can use immediately, both in the classroom and in their day-to-day work.

STUDENT'S BOOK

The *Student's Book* pack

The *Student's Book* pack offers a blend of classroom teaching and self-study, with an emphasis on flexibility and time-efficiency. Each of the 8 *Student's Book* units provides around four hours of classroom material with the potential for two to three hours of additional study using other materials in the pack.

The materials that support the *Student's Book* units are:
- *Viewpoint* video lessons
- Practice files
- Progress tests
- Photocopiable worksheets
- *Online practice*

More information on all of these materials and how to use them can be found later in these Introduction pages.

Key features of a unit

Starting point

Each unit opens with some lead-in questions to raise awareness of, and interest in, the unit theme. Use these questions to help you establish what students already know about the topic and how it relates to their own working lives. These questions can usually be discussed as a class or in small groups.

Working with words

This first main section introduces key vocabulary in a variety of ways, including authentic reading texts, listening texts and visuals. Students are also encouraged to look at how different forms of words (verbs, adjectives and nouns) can be built from the same root, or to look at common combinations (e.g. verb + noun, adjective + noun) that will help them to expand their personal lexicon more rapidly. This section also offers opportunities to work on your students' reading and listening skills.

Language at work

The grammar is looked at from a communicative point of view; this will meet your students' expectations with regard to learning form and meaning, but also reminds them how the grammar they need to learn commonly occurs in business and work situations. The *Language point* highlights the target grammar structures, which are then practised in authentic work contexts.

Practically speaking

This section looks at various practical aspects of everyday communication and social interaction – for example, *Days and times, Months and dates* – as well as useful ways that we use language in communication, such as *this, that, these* and *those*.

Business communication

In the earlier units, this section focuses on social encounters (saying hello and goodbye, meeting people) and practical situations where information needs to be exchanged – for example, taking and leaving a message, accepting and declining an invitation, giving instructions. A lot of this information is exchanged on the phone and by email, which provides particularly useful practice for students at this level. Typically, the section begins with students listening to an example situation (a meeting, a social encounter, a phone call). They focus on *Key expressions* which are listed on the page. Students are then given the opportunity to practise these in various controlled and more open work-related tasks.

Tips

Throughout each unit, there are short, practical tips with useful language points arising from a particular section or exercise.

Talking point

Most units end with a fluency task or game. This gives students an opportunity to recycle the language from the unit, demonstrate progress, and use their knowledge and ideas to resolve an authentic problem or issue. The *Talking points* have been compiled using authentic contexts in a way that connects with the unit theme. The content is accessible, and preparation time is minimized by including only as much information as can be assimilated relatively quickly in class.

The *Talking point* follows a three-part structure: Input (a short text, listening or infographic), Discussion, Task.

Note that in some units, the *Talking point* format is presented as a game. This is designed to be fun and is aimed at recycling the language from the unit.

Viewpoint

After every four units there is a two-page *Viewpoint* video lesson. The topic of the *Viewpoint* lesson relates to a theme from the preceding units and includes interviews and case studies of real companies. Each *Viewpoint* has a number of short videos and is divided into three or four sections. Key words and phrases are then introduced before students watch the main video section. Here, students can develop listening and note-taking skills with language presented in an authentic context. Each lesson ends with activities to give students speaking practice discussing the topic of the lesson.

Additional material

At the back of the *Student's Book*, you will find the following sections.

Practice files

These provide unit-by-unit support for your classroom work. Each file provides additional practice of target language from the three main unit sections, *Working with words, Language at work* and *Business communication*. This can be used in two ways:

For extra practice in class – refer students to this section for more controlled practice of new vocabulary, grammar or key expressions before moving to the next stage. The optimum point at which to do this is indicated by cross references in the *Student's Book* unit and the teaching notes in this book.

For self-study – students can complete and self-check the exercises for review and revision outside class.

Answers for the *Practice file* exercises appear on pages 61–64 of this book.

Communication activities

Additional information for pairwork and group activities.

Audio scripts

TEACHER'S BOOK

What's in each unit?

Unit content
This provides an overview of the main aims and objectives of the unit.

Context
This section not only provides information on the teaching points covered in the unit, but also offers some background information on the main business theme of the unit, and its importance in the current business world. If you are less familiar with the world of business, you will find this section especially helpful to read before starting a unit.

Teaching notes and answers
Notes on managing the *Student's Book* exercises and various activities are given throughout, with suggested variations that you might like to try. You will find comprehensive answers to all *Student's Book* exercises, as well as notes on possible responses to discussion questions.

One-to-one
In general, you will find that *Business Result Second Edition* can be used with any size of class. However, with one-to-one students you will find that activities which have been designed with groups of students in mind will need some adaptation. The *Teacher's Book* provides suggestions for how to adapt group work activities successfully for one-to-one classes.

Pre-work learners
Although most users of *Business Result Second Edition* will be students who are already in work, you may also be teaching classes of students who have little or no experience of the business world. The *Teacher's Book* provides suggestions for how to adapt certain questions or tasks in the book to their needs, and extra notes are given for these types of learners.

Extension
With some students it may be appropriate to extend an exercise in some way or relate the language point more specifically to a particular group of students. Suggestions on how to do this are given where appropriate.

Extra activity
If you have time or would like to develop further areas of language competence, extra activities are suggested where they naturally follow the order of activities in the *Student's Book*. For example, if your students need writing practice or need to build more confidence with speaking, extra follow-up ideas may be provided.

Alternative
With some students it may be preferable to approach an activity in a different way, depending on their level or their interests. These options are provided where appropriate.

Pronunciation
Tips on teaching pronunciation and helping students improve their intelligibility are provided where there is a logical need for them. These often appear where new vocabulary is taught, or for making key expressions sound more natural and fluent.

USING THE COURSE

How to use *Business Result Second Edition* to fit <u>your</u> teaching context
Business Result Second Edition provides all the flexibility you need as a teacher. The syllabus and content has been carefully designed so that it can be used either from start to finish, or in a modular way, allowing you to tailor the course to suit your and your students' needs.

Using the course from start to finish
You can, of course, use *Business Result Second Edition* conventionally, starting at *Unit 1* and working your way through each unit in turn. If you do so, you will find it works well. Each section of the unit is related thematically to the others, and there is a degree of recycling and a steady progression towards overall competence, culminating in the *Talking point*. Timing will inevitably vary, but allow approximately four classroom hours for each unit. You will need more time if you intend to do the *Practice file* activities in class.

The 'flexible' option
Business Result Second Edition is written in a way that recognizes that many business English courses vary greatly in length. With this in mind, teachers can use *Business Result Second Edition* in a modular way. Although each unit has a logical progression, you will find that all the sections are essentially free-standing and can be used independently of the rest of the unit.

This modular approach provides the flexibility that business English teachers need when planning their course. Teachers might want to choose the sections or unit topics that are the most relevant and interesting to them and their students.

Online practice and teacher resources

For students

The *Online practice* gives your students additional language practice of the *Student's Book* content. For more information, see page 3 of the *Student's Book*.

For teachers

As well as providing access to all of the student online practice exercises, the Learning Management System (LMS) provides an invaluable and time-saving feature for teachers.

You can monitor your students' progress and all of their results at the touch of a button. You can also print off and use student reports on their progress.

A training guide for how to use the LMS can be found in the teacher resources in the *Online practice*.

Downloadable resources for teachers

In the teacher resources in the *Online practice* are a number of downloadable resources for teachers to use to complement the *Student's Book*. These include:

- Photocopiable worksheets for every unit
- Progress tests for every unit
- Revision game
- Business cards for role-plays
- Class audio
- Class video

Photocopiable worksheets

New for *Business Result Second Edition* are the photocopiable worksheets. These provide extra communicative practice, often in the form of a game, for every *Working with words*, *Language at work* and *Business communication* section from the *Student's Book*.

There are suggestions in the *Teacher's Book* for when to use these worksheets in class. All of the worksheets, as well as the answer key, can be downloaded and photocopied from the teacher resources in the *Online practice*.

Photocopiable Progress tests

These can be administered at the end of each unit in order to assess your students' progress and allow you, the student, or the head of training to keep track of students' overall ability.

Each test is divided into two sections. The first section tests the vocabulary, grammar and key expressions from the unit. This section is scored out of 30 and students will need about 30 minutes to complete the questions.

The second section is a speaking test. In this section students are given a speaking task that resembles one of the speaking activities in the unit. These are mostly set up as pairwork activities in the form of role-plays, discussions or presentations.

Marking criteria is provided to help you assess students' performance in the speaking test. It requires students to perform five functions in the speaking test, and you can grade each of the five stages using a scoring system of 0, 1 or 2, giving a final score out of ten.

The speaking test role-plays can also be used as extra classroom practice without necessarily making use of the marking criteria.

All of the tests, and the answer keys, can be downloaded from the teacher resources in the *Online practice*.

Revision game

The *Revision game* provides the chance to review all the language taught in the 8 units of *Business Result Second Edition Starter*.

This can be downloaded and photocopied from the teacher resources in the *Online practice*.

Business cards

There is a set of downloadable business cards in the teacher resources in the *Online practice*.

The business cards are particularly useful to use in role-play situations from the *Student's Book* if you have students from the same company and they are required to exchange information about their company. You will find suggestions of when to use the business cards in the teacher notes of the *Teacher's Book*.

Class audio and video

All of the class audio and the videos for the *Viewpoint* lessons can be streamed or downloaded from the teacher resources in the *Online practice*.

Alternatively, class audio can be played from the audio CD and the videos can be played from the DVD that is found in the *Teacher's Book* pack.

How to access the *Online practice*

For students

Students use the access card on the inside front cover of the *Student's Book*. This contains an access code to unlock the content in the *Online practice*.

For teachers

Teachers need to go to **www.oxfordlearn.com** and either register or sign in. Members of the Oxford Teacher's Club can use their existing sign in details.

Then click on **Register an organization** and follow the instructions. Note that if you are not part of an organization, or you don't have an authorization code from your institution, you will need to click on **Apply for an organization account**. You will then be asked to supply some information. If you don't have an institution, then put your own name next to Institution name.

Teacher's website

Additional teacher resources can be found at **www.oup.com/elt/teacher/businessresult**

1 You

Unit content

By the end of this unit, students will be able to
- introduce themselves
- talk about jobs
- ask about names and jobs
- say the alphabet and spell names
- meet people in different business contexts.

Context

This unit provides beginner students with the key words and expressions they'll need to talk about themselves at work. In particular, the language will help them with introducing themselves and their colleagues in a variety of business situations. They also begin practising spelling and saying the alphabet.

The key business topic in the unit is jobs and job titles. To reflect the modern business world, job titles have become highly specialized in recent years, so students need plenty of practice at saying what they do and understanding what others are responsible for. This unit gives them their first opportunity to do this in English.

The *Language at work* section in this unit is the first of three (in *Units 1* to *3*) that presents students with the different forms of the verb *to be* in the present simple. *Unit 1* introduces the *I / you* form in the affirmative, negative, and interrogative. Students practise using the structures by asking and answering questions about their names and jobs. This is then supported by work done on spelling names in *Practically speaking*.

The *Business communication* section provides different ways of saying hello and goodbye, and also key expressions for meeting and introducing people. Students listen to model versions before role-playing similar situations.

The final activity brings together all the new language from the unit in a *Talking point* where students work in groups of three and practise conversations at a conference. After completing their first unit of *Business Result Second Edition Starter*, students should feel like they have already communicated in English in an authentic situation.

Starting point

As this is a beginner course, you might have students in the class who don't know any English at all, and there could be some students who know one or two words and phrases such as *Hello* and *My name's* … If you think your class will never have seen the questions in *Starting point* before, you could begin the lesson with books closed.

Gesture to yourself and say your full name. Gesture to each student one by one and elicit their names until everyone has introduced themselves. You could also ask students to write their names on a name badge or piece of card to display. Next, ask students to open their books and read the first question *What's your name?*

Model the question for the class and answer it with your name so they understand the question. Then ask the students the question and elicit the answer. Note that you don't need students to ask the question at this stage of the course. They just need to recognize its meaning. Next, model the second question and gesture to yourself giving the answer (*I'm a teacher*).

Because students will need to say their job titles in response to this question and later on in the unit, it's a good idea to try and find out what your students do beforehand. Many job titles can be quite complex so, if possible, choose generic titles such as *engineer* or *manager* at this stage of the lesson and teach each student to say their own job. If necessary, have the jobs written on name badges or pieces of card for reference.

PRE-WORK LEARNERS Teach the pre-work learners to say *I'm a student* in response to the second question.

Working with words

Exercise 1

▶ **1.1** Point to the pictures in the book and read the rubric aloud. It's useful at this early stage of a beginner course to establish actions with the instructions. For example, with this rubric *Listen and read*, touch your ear when you say the word *Listen* and point at your eyes when you say *read*. (For the instruction to *speak*, point at the mouth, and for *write*, make the movement of a pen across paper or move your fingers as if typing on a keyboard.)

EXTENSION You could show that the meaning of these words in the sentences are essentially the same by writing this on the board:

Hello = Hi

I'm = My name's

Exercise 2

▶ **1.1** Students listen and repeat the conversations in **1**. At this level, you can play the listening more than once. Students need to hear the model version a lot. You also need to drill the phrases, so chorally drill the class and drill individuals.

Exercise 3

While students work in pairs using their own names, monitor and check that everyone understands what is expected and that they can clearly introduce themselves. If necessary, ask for pairs to perform their conversations to you and the rest of the class.

Exercise 4

Gesture that you want everyone to stand up by doing it yourself and raising your hands palm up. If you are teaching in a classroom culture where students are not used to standing up and walking around, you might need to spend a little time at this stage making sure everyone understands the idea. If it's a very large class, you might divide students up into working groups of six to eight.

ONE-TO-ONE One option is to bring in a collection of real business cards or download the *Business cards* in the teacher resources in *the Online practice*. Pretend you are the people on those cards. Take turns to pick up a card and introduce yourself as that person.

Exercise 5

▶ **1.2** Play the listening of the six job titles and students read. If you have any students in the class with these actual job titles, ask the question *What's your job?* and elicit the job title on the page again.

Exercise 6

▶ **1.3** Students practise the pronunciation of the job words. This is the first time many students will have encountered the idea that words have stress patterns, so be prepared to play the listening a few times, or drill the words yourself.

EXTENSION A simple extension task is to write the six job words on pieces of card and the six stress patterns on other pieces of card. Each pair of students receives a set of these cards and tries to match each job card with the card with the correct stress pattern.

PRONUNCIATION If your students all said their job titles in *Starting point*, write these on the board and mark the word stress. Then drill the class in saying their job titles with the correct word stress.

Exercise 7

▶ **1.4** Play the listening at least twice. The first time, students should just listen and read. Then play it again and they fill in the gaps.

> **Answers**
> 1 human resources manager
> 2 finance director
> 3 IT technician
> 4 office assistant

Exercise 8

Before students start to create their own conversations, refer them to the explanation of *a / an* in the *Tip*. To expand the rule, you might want to write the letters *a, e, i, o, u* on the board and explain that these need *an* before them. Point out the exception of words beginning with *u* that have a /j/ sound at the beginning, e.g. *a university*. As an extension task, refer back to the list of jobs in **5** and ask students to identify whether they need *a* or *an*. Note also that **4** in the *Practice file* is an activity with *a / an* and students could do this activity now.

Students work in pairs and read the two conversations in **7** aloud. Then they can swap roles and repeat the conversations.

Further practice

If students need more practice, go to *Practice file 1* on page 56 of the *Student's Book*.

> **EXTRA ACTIVITY**
> This is the first time in the book that students see a cross reference to a *Practice file*. You won't always choose to interrupt the lesson by turning to this section in the book, but as this is the first lesson, you might want to show students where they can find extra practice to do in class or for homework.

Exercise 9

Students need to insert their own names and jobs into the two conversations. With weaker groups, they could write out the conversations in full with their names and jobs before speaking.

As this is the first lesson, most of your feedback to the class will be very positive and reassuring. With beginner level students in the first lesson, praise is crucial. While monitoring the final task, you will need to remind them of certain words. You might also choose to help with word stress and with stronger students, you can correct use of *a / an* before a job title where necessary.

PRE-WORK LEARNERS Write some job titles on separate pieces of paper. Take the job titles from **5** and any other job titles that you think they are familiar with. Give each student a piece of paper with a job title on and they pretend it's their own job. You could also use this activity if you have a class where everyone has the same kind of job.

Photocopiable worksheet

Download and photocopy *Unit 1 Working with words worksheet* from the teacher resources in the *Online practice*.

Language at work

Exercise 1

▶ **1.5** After students listen and read, you could ask them to circle *'m* and *'re* in the conversation to prepare for the next activity. If necessary, model the task by writing a sentence on the board with *'m* and *'re*, and then circling the verbs. For example:

Ⓘ*m Jacob*

YouⓇⓔ*Alice.*

Exercise 2

Students write the missing verb forms in the table in the *Language point*.

Answers

Positive	Negative
I'm Jacob.	**I'm** not Alice.
You**'re** Alice.	You're not Maria.

PRONUNCIATION Students need to practise the contracted forms that occur with the subject and the verb in the *Language point*. So drill the four example sentences in the table in **2**.

Grammar reference

If students need more information, go to *Grammar reference* on page 57 of the *Student's Book*.

Exercise 3

Put students into groups of four and they read aloud. If you have drilled the contracted forms, monitor for this use.

ONE-TO-ONE Ask the student to read what Jacob says, and you take the other roles.

Exercise 4

▶ **1.6** Play the listening twice so that students can listen once and then listen and write the next time. They can also refer to the grammar table which shows the *you* question form and the short answers.

Refer students to the *Tip* so they can see how and when we use the full form and the contracted form.

Answers
1 Are
2 am
3 'm not
4 'm

Exercise 5

Students practise using the full form and the contracted form in a simple question / answer speaking task.

EXTENSION If students seem confident with the forms, they can continue the activity in **5** a few more times by using more job titles from the previous *Working with words* lesson or using their own job titles.

Further practice

If students need more practice, go to *Practice file 1* on page 57 of the *Student's Book*.

Exercise 6

▶ **1.7** This listening presents a model version of the conversation practice that students will have in the activity that follows.

Answer
3   Enzo Silva (Sales Manager).

Exercise 7

Students play a guessing game with the four name badges. Check that the students are using and saying the contracted forms and full forms correctly. Drill on the spot if necessary.

EXTENSION   With larger classes, students might still not know everyone else's name and job yet, so this is a simple way to get to know them and to practise the target grammar. Ask everyone to stand and walk around the room. Students have to go up to each other and see if they can remember each other's names and jobs. If after three attempts they don't guess correctly, they can ask *What's your name?* or *What's your job?* End the activity by going round the class and finding out if people can remember the names and jobs of everyone else in the room. (It's a good chance for you to check you know all the students' names too!)

EXTRA ACTIVITY
Write everyone's job on separate pieces of paper. Deal these out randomly so everyone has the name of a different job. They all stand and walk around trying to find the student with the job written on their card by asking *Are you a / an …?*

Photocopiable worksheet
Download and photocopy *Unit 1 Language at work worksheet* from the teacher resources in the *Online practice*.

Practically speaking

Exercise 1

▶ **1.8** If you are teaching monolingual groups of students or one-to-one, how you approach saying the alphabet will depend on the first language of your students. You will need to take longer with students who use a different script in their own language.

EXTENSION   As a class, drill the 26 letters in different ways. You can go round the group in a circle with each student saying the next letter. Alternatively, let students work on their own or in pairs and practise saying the alphabet quietly for a while. Note also that the *Practice file* includes a useful activity focusing on the fact that certain letters have similar vowel sounds. This might be a good moment to set the activity before moving on.

EXTRA ACTIVITY
Ask everyone to stand and organize themselves in alphabetical order according to the first letter of their first names. Then repeat the activity according to the first letter of their surnames. This is a good communicative task to establish the idea of an order in the alphabet and to use spelling to complete a task.

Exercise 2

Students look at the image of the keyboard and say the rows of letters. Because they are in a different order than in **1**, it's a useful way to review the pronunciation.

Exercise 3

▶ **1.9** Students listen to a conversation in an office and write in the missing names. Play once, then let students compare their answers with a partner before playing again to check.

The contacts list introduces the words *first name* and *surname* and these words also appear in the listening, so this is a good moment to clarify the meaning.

Answers
1   Azikiwe
2   Gabryjela

EXTENSION   For further speaking practice, put students in pairs and tell them to turn to the audio script on page 76. They can read the conversation in listening 1.9 between the Assistant and the Manager. It's a simple way to practise more spelling and it also introduces the useful phrase *Can you spell that?* in context.

Exercise 4

Students practise the conversation with the names in **3**, but you could also extend the activity by having them spell the four names listed in **6** of *Language at work*.

Further practice
If students need more practice, go to *Practice file 1* on page 57 of the *Student's Book*.

Exercise 5

Students can work with one partner to carry out this task and then swap partners so they get lots of practice at spelling different first names and surnames.

Business communication

Exercise 1

▶ **1.10** Students match the conversations to the pictures. The listening introduces the phrases *Good morning* and *Good afternoon*, and these are illustrated by the clocks in the pictures. Either before or after the listening, introduce the two ways of greeting by drawing clocks on the board and explaining when morning ends or afternoon starts. You could also draw clocks to teach the phrases *Good evening* and *Good night*.

ALTERNATIVE Before listening to the three conversations, ask students to look at the three pictures. Students could suggest short conversations between the people using the language from the previous four pages.

Answers
a 2
b 1
c 3

Exercise 2

Students can do this on their own and then check with their partner. Note that students might try to translate words and expressions such as *Nice to meet you,* or they may ask why we reply in a certain way such as *Nice to meet you too*. On the *Business communication* pages, try to teach the language as expressions and avoid analysing the sentences in terms of isolated words or looking at the grammar. If you speak the students' first language, you can point out that in their own language they will have fixed expressions in social situations that can't always be translated literally.

Exercise 3

▶ **1.11** Play the listening to check the answers. Then play it again so they can repeat the sentences.

Answers
1 b
2 e
3 a
4 c
5 d

EXTENSION In groups of three, students could practise reading the conversations in audio script 1.11 on page 76 aloud to build their confidence.

Exercise 4

Do the first sentence together to demonstrate what to do. Students can then either work individually or in pairs to correct the remaining sentences.

Once they have finished, refer students to the *Key expressions* to help them check their answers. This will also draw their attention to other ways of saying hello, meeting people, introducing other people, and saying goodbye.

Answers
1 Good afternoon. ~~Am~~ **Are** you Jacob?
2 Nice to ~~meeting~~ **meet** you, Sally.
3 ~~Seeing~~ **See** you soon.
4 This ~~are~~ **is** Kasia.
5 I**'m** Franco. Nice to meet you.
6 **A** Are you Mara?
   B Yes, I ~~'m~~ **am**.

Further practice

If students need more practice, go to *Practice file 1* on page 56 of the *Student's Book*.

Exercise 5

Students work in threes and use the pictures as prompts for speaking. They can repeat the activity a few times by swapping roles. As they become more confident, suggest they cover the *Key expressions* and other activities to prevent reading the expressions and to test their memories.

ONE-TO-ONE For **5** and **6**, you could take on the parts of different people, or you could give the student different names and job titles to use. You could find these by downloading the *Business cards* from the teacher resources in the *Online practice*.

Exercise 6

End this section with students standing and practising the language with the whole class. To add variation, give out new identities and job titles to students so that they pretend to be someone different.

Monitor for the correct use of different expressions. Give lots of praise afterwards and drill any expressions which are causing difficulty.

ONE-TO-ONE If possible, ask another person to come to the class to help practise introductions. Otherwise, you and the student can just introduce yourselves.

Photocopiable worksheet

Download and photocopy *Unit 1 Business communication worksheet* from the teacher resources in the *Online practice*.

Talking point

This flow chart activity is a way of reviewing all the vocabulary, grammar, and expressions from the unit in the context of attending a business conference. Not all your students will attend a conference, but it could be any situation where students have to meet people and make conversation about themselves and their job.

Exercise 1

Students work in groups of three and can either sit or stand in a circle. They begin by completing the expressions in the conversation. This can be done orally or they can write the missing words. Before they start the conversation properly, you could go through it as a whole class to check everyone has prepared a correct conversation.

Exercise 2

Students repeat the conversation by changing roles. As they become more confident, they could cover the prompts for their part to add to the level of difficulty until they can say the words from memory.

Early on in the task, allow students time to make mistakes and repeat the conversation. But in **2**, start to correct pronunciation and check that students are using the verbs *'m* and *'re* correctly as well as *a / an* + job title.

ONE-TO-ONE Allocate Student A to your student and you play the parts of B and C. Then swap roles and repeat so the student is Student B and you are A and C. Do this as many times as necessary. Then close the book and try to carry out a similar conversation as if the student is meeting someone for the first time at a real conference.

Progress test

Download and photocopy *Unit 1 Progress test* and *Speaking test* from the teacher resources in the *Online practice*.

2 Company

Unit content

By the end of this unit, students will be able to

- talk about companies and countries
- ask about people and companies
- say numbers 0–9
- start a phone call.

Context

In this unit, students start to learn how to talk about their companies and countries. The unit provides key language for describing a range of companies and the location of their different operations, including their head offices. Students also learn how to ask other people about their companies. This allows them to operate at a basic level when interacting with clients and colleagues.

In *Language at work*, students extend their use of the verb *to be* to deal with the *he / she / it* form. Using this, they can talk about other businesses and where other people are based. Students are also introduced to using the numbers 0–9 in a range of contexts, including phone numbers and flight numbers.

Students practise starting and answering phone calls with basic phrases. They also find out how to ask to speak to someone else. If they receive calls, they also begin to deal with callers. *Business communication* offers students lots of practice with making calls and it will be very motivating for your students to see that they can already complete a basic workplace task with only limited English.

In the *Talking point*, students make short conversations to practise greetings, asking about companies, and phone call phrases.

Starting point

It will be helpful to bring in a few business cards to the lesson for reference. You can also refer students to the business cards on the page. Show students a business card and ask them what's on it.

For added help, you can write these words on the board:

Name   Company name   Job title   Address   Phone number   Other information?

Give each student a business card and ask them to find the items from the board on their card.

Then, for the second question, ask students to present their own cards.

PRE-WORK LEARNERS As pre-work learners are unlikely to have their own cards (though some might), you can give them a business card that you've brought in and ask them to present it. You could also hand out blank pieces of card and ask your learners to design their own business cards and then present them to the class.

Working with words

Exercise 1
▶ **2.1** You could play the listening twice. Ask students to listen to and read the conversation between Saleh and Ricardo. Then play it again and students complete the business card.

> **Answers**
> 1 Engineer
> 2 Zain
> 3 Kuwait

EXTENSION Put students into pairs and ask them to read the conversation in **1** aloud.

Exercise 2
▶ **2.2** Students could read the cards first and try to predict which company is likely to be in which location indicated on the card. Then they listen and check. You could also check their pronunciation of the three job titles (*Manager, Marketing Assistant, Engineer*) to review the work on word stress with job titles in Unit 1.

> **Answers**
> 1 Santander
> 2 Asiana Airlines
> 3 Petrobras

Exercise 3
Students work in pairs and practise the A/B conversation. Monitor and drill any parts of the conversation as necessary. With smaller classes, students could stand and mill around the room, introducing themselves to everyone in the class using the same conversation.

EXTENSION Ask the pairs of students to look back at the conversation between Saleh and Ricardo in **1** and create a similar conversation using their own names, company names, and jobs.

PRE-WORK LEARNERS Once again, you can carry out the speaking activity in **3** by giving your students a business card and they play the part of the person on that card, or they create their own business cards with imaginary company names.

Exercise 4
Students use the map to point at the location of their head offices. Stronger students could say the names of the locations before the next activity. You could also vary the activity so that students point to where they live or where they come from.

Exercise 5
Students match the countries to the parts of the map.

> **Answers**
> 1 the USA
> 2 Brazil
> 3 Spain
> 4 Germany
> 5 Saudi Arabia
> 6 Kuwait
> 7 China
> 8 South Korea
> 9 Japan

Exercise 6
▶ **2.3** As students listen and repeat, monitor for correct stress. Afterwards, work on any difficulties remedially.

EXTENSION If your students' countries are not listed in **5**, write the countries on the board and mark the word stress so that they can learn to pronounce them correctly.

Exercise 7
▶ **2.4** Before listening, students could guess at the countries and places according to the names of the people. Then they listen to check.

> **Answers**
>
> | Saleh | Alex | Jae Min | Ricardo |
> |---|---|---|---|
> | *Saudi Arabia* | the USA | South Korea | Brazil |
> | Kuwait | Spain | Seoul | Rio de Janeiro |

Exercise 8
▶ **2.4** After students listen and complete the questions and answers, they could check by reading the audio script on page 76. Students could also work in pairs and read the questions and answers aloud.

> **Answers**
> 1 I'm from
> 2 What's, company
> 3 Where's
> 4 Where, work

Exercise 9
Help students to complete the three sentences by providing any necessary words. Then ask students to practise saying the three sentences to themselves or to their partners. (See notes for pre-work learners after **10**.)

Exercise 10
Students work in pairs and ask and answer the questions. Then they can change partners and repeat the conversations.

After the pairwork activity, draw their attention to the *Tip* box, which focuses on the use of *and* to join two sentences. Students could make their own sentences about their companies and their head offices using *and*.

PRE-WORK LEARNERS For students at university or college, you could provide this alternative language on the board to replace the sentences and questions in **9** and **10**:

I study at _____ .
My university / college is in _____ .
What's your university?
Where's your university / college?

Further practice
If students need more practice, go to *Practice file 2* on page 58 of the *Student's Book*.

Exercise 11
Put students in pairs and ask them to turn to the pages indicated. Allow time for students to read their information and understand that they will have to ask and answer questions. You could model one or two questions with a student so that everyone is clear about the task. This

task may also require students to ask for the spelling of certain words, so you might want to check that everyone remembers how to ask for spelling from *Unit 1*. You could also review spelling the alphabet with the class beforehand if necessary.

Monitor for correct question forms and correct word stress with the names of countries. If students are trying to spell words, you may like to re-drill some of the more difficult letters of the alphabet for most learners, such as *a*, *e*, and *i*.

EXTENSION To extend the task and provide further useful practice, students could repeat the information gap activity in **11** by swapping roles.

Photocopiable worksheet

Download and photocopy *Unit 2 Working with words worksheet* from the teacher resources in the *Online practice*.

Language at work

Exercise 1

Students read the four emails and complete sentences 1 and 2 for general comprehension.

Answers
1 Rio de Janeiro
2 on holiday

Exercise 2

Students underline *is* or *isn't* in the emails.

Answers
<u>Is</u> Camilla Branco in the Recife office?
No, she <u>isn't</u>. She'<u>s</u> in the head office in Rio.
Thanks. <u>Is</u> the number 0055 3064 4758?
Yes, it <u>is</u>. But she <u>isn't</u> in the office now. She'<u>s</u> on holiday.

Exercise 3

Students complete the table in the *Language point*. After this, it may be helpful to show students that this is a form of the verb *to be*. You could refer students back to *Unit 1* and the forms of *to be* for *I* and *you* to show the connection.

Answers

Positive	Negative	Questions	Short answers
He / She / It **is** (**'s**) in the office.	He / She / It **isn't** in Recife.	**Is** he / she / it in Rio?	Yes, he / she / it **is**. No, he / she / it **isn't**.

Grammar reference

If students need more information, go to *Grammar reference* on page 59 of the *Student's Book*.

Exercise 4

▶ **2.5** Students write in the correct form before listening to check. With weaker classes, you could play the listening and students write in what they hear.

Before moving on to **5**, refer students to the *Tip* so they can see how and when we use the full form and the contracted form. Use the opportunity to drill the pronunciation of the contracted form '*s*.

Answers
1 is
2 Is
3 isn't
4 is
5 Is
6 is

Exercise 5

Students read the conversation aloud. Check for correct pronunciation of any contracted forms such as *It's* and *isn't*.

Ask students to work in pairs and write a similar conversation with their own companies and locations. As they write, check that they use the correct forms of the verb *to be*. Afterwards, ask them to read their conversations aloud to the class.

Further practice
If students need more practice, go to *Practice file 2* on page 59 of the *Student's Book*.

Exercise 6
Each student has a map showing information about three people. They have to find out more information about three other people by asking their partner *Is he / she …?* questions. Note that the questions have short *Yes / No* answers.

Listen for the correct use of *is / isn't* as well as good pronunciation of the country names. After any necessary feedback, students could repeat the task by changing partners and swapping roles.

Photocopiable worksheet
Download and photocopy *Unit 2 Language at work worksheet* from the teacher resources in the *Online practice*.

Practically speaking

Exercise 1
▶ **2.6** Students listen and repeat the numbers 0–9. Afterwards, you can drill the numbers by going round the class with each student saying the next number in the sequence.

Students may find it useful to refer to the *Tip* at any time during this section, but in particular make sure they notice that we can say the number 0 in two ways. Generally, it's helpful for students to learn to use *zero*, as in international business this avoids misunderstanding where *oh* is not universally used. However, they need to be aware that they might hear the number said as *oh*, especially with British English native speakers. If you have sports enthusiasts in the class, you might also want to teach them the word *nil* for referring to scores.

Exercise 2
▶ **2.7** Students listen to some numbers and circle the numbers on the phone.

Answer
0 7 8 5 4 2

Exercise 3
▶ **2.8** Now they listen for the passcode and write the digits.

Answer
6 7 2 0

Exercise 4
▶ **2.9** The next listening is more difficult because the numbers appear in a sentence rather than in isolation. However, each number is repeated twice in the sentence.

Answers
1 3710
2 2828
3 4162 7409 3708 2358
4 654218792

Write the numbers 0–9 around the board. Ask everyone to choose any four numbers and write them down. Then explain that you will call the numbers out in any order. If a student hears one of his/her numbers, they cross it out. The first student to hear all four of his/her numbers wins. You can then repeat the activity, but ask the winning student to call the numbers out. It's a simple but motivating activity which can be continued with lots of students calling out the numbers. With larger classes, you could set up the same activity among groups of four to six students.

Further practice
If students need more practice, go to *Practice file 2* on page 59 of the *Student's Book*.

Exercise 5

Students work on their own and write numbers in the *You* column. If they don't have an extension number, they can make one up or ignore that part of the table.

PRE-WORK LEARNERS Students can complete the table with numbers for their college or university, and an extension for a department, or they can use the company where a family member or friend works.

Exercise 6

Now working in pairs, they dictate their numbers in **5** to their partners, who write them down. To extend the task, students could stand and walk around the class, giving their numbers to one another.

Business communication

ALTERNATIVE If you have false beginners in the group, you could ask them to look at the picture of the receptionist answering the call and elicit what she might be saying. Find out if students are aware of any phrases we use to answer the phone.

Exercise 1

▶ 2.10 Students listen and identify if Aitur is there. If students need clarification of the phrase *Is Aitur there?*, sketch two offices on the board. In one, draw a picture of a man and leave the other empty. Ask students *Is Aitur in his office or not in his office?*

Exercise 2

▶ 2.10 Students could try to reorder the conversation before listening and then listen to check their answers.

Note that the grammatical explanation of the modal *can* is not given until Unit 6. Avoid having to explain it at this stage and present it only as a fixed expression that we use for polite requests.

Answers
1 Good morning. Inditex Spain.
3 Yes, of course. One moment.
4 Thanks.
2 Good morning. Can I speak to Aitur Garitano, please?

Exercise 3

To add authenticity to the conversation, students can sit back to back so they aren't looking at each other. Or students could call each other with their mobiles. Ask them to practise reading the conversation twice and taking on the role of receptionist and caller.

Exercise 4

▶ 2.11 Play the listening twice so students listen and tick and then listen again to be certain.

Answers
1 NO
2 YES

Exercise 5

▶ 2.11 Students listen again and match the questions and responses.

Answers
1 c
2 a
3 b

EXTENSION Students could check their answers to **5** by reading the audio script on page 77. Then put them in pairs and ask them to read the two conversations aloud as they did in **3** to build their confidence for the freer practice activity that follows.

Further practice

If students need more practice, go to *Practice file 2* on page 58 of the *Student's Book*.

Exercise 6

Students role-play a series of phone conversations between a caller and a receptionist. The caller plays him/herself and chooses a person in the picture. The receptionist looks to see if the person is in his/her office and responds appropriately.

Give feedback on correct use of the *Key expressions* and, if you have focused on polite intonation, give praise and/or drill them again where necessary. Many students will appreciate having plenty of time for practising the language of making phone calls, so it's often a good idea to give the feedback and then have students swap their partners and repeat the activity.

ONE-TO-ONE Throughout this *Business communication* page, you will need to do all the role-plays with the student. This could easily be done with real phones, calling from separate locations. If possible, record the phone calls with your student and play them back afterwards. This is a useful way to give feedback and for the student to hear their progress.

Photocopiable worksheet

Download and photocopy *Unit 2 Business communication worksheet* from the teacher resources in the *Online practice*.

Talking point

The company game brings together all the language from the unit and revises it. You can use it straight after you have completed the unit, but you could also return to it again at a later date for revision practice.

Put students in pairs. They can each use a counter to move across the board (such as a coin). There are different ways that students can move across the board. They can work alone and match the four expressions by saying each one in turn. Alternatively, they work in pairs and take turns to say the next part of the conversation as if they are role-playing it.

Answers

Hello, are you Rafael? / Yes, I am. / My name's Sonia. / Nice to meet you, Sonia.
What's your company? / It's Petrobras. / Where's your head office? / It's in Brazil.
What's your name? / Haruka Naito. / Where are you from, Haruka? / I'm from Japan.
Is that Philippe? / No, it's Remi. / Is Philippe there? / Sure, one moment.
Good morning. Inditex. / Hello. Can I speak to Maya? / I'm sorry, she's out. / OK. Thanks.

EXTENSION Once students are familiar with the conversations, they could extend the practice by doing the following: one student sits with their book closed and the other student reads out phrases from the pink or blue squares. The student with the book closed has to give an appropriate response and gets a point for every correct answer (either from the game or one of their own).

Progress test

Download and photocopy *Unit 2 Progress test* and *Speaking test* from the teacher resources in the *Online practice*.

3 Workplace

Unit content

By the end of this unit, students will be able to

- talk about their company and their workplace
- ask questions about the company and the workplace
- say email and website addresses
- email a request.

Context

In this unit, students learn how to describe their companies in more detail and they also start to talk about their workplaces in detail. The language in *Working with words* allows them to be specific about places in the company, and they are also introduced to adjectives for the first time. This language will be useful when presenting their company and for making small talk about their working lives.

After the *I / you / he / she / it* forms of the verb *to be* in *Units 1* and *2*, the *Language at work* in this unit completes the grammar point with *we / they + to be*, so that students can practise and revise all the forms. It also extends the *Wh-* questions from *What* and *Where* to include *Who*, so now students can ask about people as well as objects and places.

Practically speaking builds on the previous two units, which introduced spelling and numbers, to deal with the necessary skill of saying email and website addresses. This leads into a more detailed look at writing emails for the first time in the book in *Business communication*. Students focus on the key structure of basic business emails and the phrases they will need to handle day-to-day email correspondence.

In the *Talking point*, students practise question and answer exchanges using *to be*.

Starting point

Students were introduced to *Where …?* questions in *Unit 2*, so this is a review. Students can work in pairs and take turns to ask each other the three questions.

PRE-WORK LEARNERS Adapt the task by writing these other options on the board:

Where is …?

- *your home*
- *your university / college*
- *your favourite place*

Working with words

Exercise 1
▶ **3.1** Allow plenty of time for students to study the information about the company Mieszanka. After they listen, you could also play the listening again and students could listen and repeat each part of the information.

Exercise 2
Students can work together to answer the questions. Note that the answers to 2–4 are Polish names, so write them on the board rather than asking students to try and give you the answer (unless you have Polish students of course!).

Answers
1 Poland
2 Katowice
3 Warsaw
4 Poznań

Exercise 3
Draw attention to the list of workplaces given in the final sentence about the new factory in Poznań in **1**, and then ask students to match the words.

Answers
1 a warehouse
2 a factory
3 a cafeteria
4 a reception
5 an office
6 a car park

Exercise 4
▶ **3.2** Students practise saying the words with the correct word stress.

Exercise 5
Students talk about the places in their own companies. If you know that your students work in different types of companies with industry-specific locations (such as laboratories or hotels), then be prepared to teach these words to individual students with the correct word stress.

PRE-WORK LEARNERS Set the students a short research task on the Internet. Ask them to choose a company and visit its website. They should list the types of places it has in the company. Alternatively, they could choose a local company they are familiar with and describe the places in the company.

Exercise 6
Before reading and answering, refer students to the list of adjectives and pictures below the question. Read them out and ask students to repeat the six adjectives. Then let them read the text again and choose the correct adjective.

Answers
1 old
2 big
3 good

Exercise 7
▶ **3.3** Students listen and write the adjective they hear.

Answers
1 small
2 old, big
3 small, good

Further practice
If students need more practice, go to *Practice file 3* on page 60 of the *Student's Book*.

Exercise 8
Before students start talking, they can spend time on their own thinking about which adjectives in **6** describe the places in the list.

The *Tip* highlights the change in word order when using adjectives with nouns. In **8**, the target sentence uses the structure of *to be* + adjective. However, students need to know that you can use an adjective before the noun. This will be of particular help to students whose first language puts the noun before the adjective (for example, Spanish).

Give feedback on the correct pronunciation of the workplaces and the adjectives. Also monitor for incorrect word order and write down any incorrect sentences. At the end, write them on the board and ask students to spot the mistakes.

PRE-WORK LEARNERS Write alternative places for students to describe on the board that you know are in their place of study. For example:
university / college cafeteria classroom car park library

EXTENSION If your students seem confident about describing the places listed, you could write other things on the board connected either with their working lives or leisure time such as:
house city or town car mobile phone laptop football team

EXTRA ACTIVITY
To provide some controlled practice with the rule in the *Tip*, tell students to do **8** again, but this time use the adjective + noun structure for each item. Note also that **3** in *Working with words* in *Practice file 3* offers further practice with this structure.

Photocopiable worksheet
Download and photocopy *Unit 3 Working with words worksheet* from the teacher resources in the *Online practice*.

Language at work

Exercise 1

This lead-in question revises the places introduced in the previous *Working with words* section. Students can work in pairs and identify the different places.

Answers
a a car park
b a reception
c a cafeteria
d an office
e a factory

EXTRA ACTIVITY
If you have time, you could also teach or elicit the words for other items in the pictures such as *desk*, *coffee machine*, *phone*, *computer*, *machine*.

Exercise 2

Students match the sentences.

Answers
1 a
2 c
3 d
4 e
5 b

Exercise 3

Before students do this activity, you could ask them to underline examples of *'re*, *are*, or *aren't* in sentences 1–5 in **2**. This draws their attention to the forms used in context before completing the table in *Language point 1*.

Answers

Positive	Negative	Question	Short answers
We / They **are** in the warehouse.	We / They **aren't** in the factory.	**Are** we / they in reception?	Yes, we / they **are**. No, we / they **aren't**.

EXTENSION Follow up this presentation by asking students which other pronoun uses the same form of the verb *to be* as *we* and *they*. (The answer is the *you* form.) Also remind them that *'re* is the contracted form of *are* and that it cannot be used in questions or short answers.

Grammar reference
If students need more information, go to *Grammar reference* on page 61 of the *Student's Book*.

Exercise 4

If you think students need time to work with the form before asking and answering questions, they could write some conversations about the pictures. Alternatively, they could work in pairs and prepare five questions. Then they could join another pair and take turns to ask and answer their questions.

Exercise 5

In **4**, students only practise the *they + to be* form. This activity is designed to make them have similar conversations, but this time they are using the *we + to be* form.

EXTENSION Stronger students could continue the conversation practice in **5** by thinking of other places. For example:

Are you in the city?
No, we aren't.
Are you in the classroom?
Yes, we are. We're students.

Exercise 6

▶ **3.4** Note that the names of the places are not said in every conversation and students will need to refer to the pictures in **1** and work out from context where the people are.

Answers
1 in reception
2 in the office
3 in the cafeteria

Exercise 7

▶ **3.4** Students match the questions and answers before listening to check.

Answers
1 c
2 a
3 b

Further practice
If students need more practice, go to *Practice file 3* on page 61 of the *Student's Book*.

Exercise 8

Students match the question word to the thing it asks about. They could do this by drawing a line in *Language point 2*.

Answers
What – a thing
Where – a place
Who – a person

Grammar reference
If students need more information, go to *Grammar reference* on page 61 of the *Student's Book*.

EXTENSION Refer students to the *Grammar reference* of *Wh-* questions followed by the verb *to be*. To review the rules of *to be*, write *you / he / she / it / we / they* on the board and ask students to say which follows a question + *'s*. (Answer: *he / she / it* form) Then ask which follows a question + *are*. (Answer: *you / we / they*)

Exercise 9

This activity provides freer practice with all the language taught in this section. Students choose the people they want to talk about in the pictures and take turns to ask and answer questions.

Initially, concentrate on students' correct use of the verb *to be* in these conversations and the right choice of *Wh-* question word. Once they are using the new grammar effectively, focus on any pronunciation issues such as word stress (and sentence stress in questions if you dealt with it earlier).

EXTENSION Normally, we use *who* to ask about a person or people, but in real English we can also use the *Who* question to find out a person's job title or position within the company. Ask students to read the *Tip* and, if you have time, ask a student *Who are they?* and point at two people in the class. The student should give their names and also say their job titles. Students can then practise similar conversations in pairs.

PRONUNCIATION For additional pronunciation work, you can look at sentence stress in question forms. Write the three questions from **7** on the board and underline the words as shown here:

What's your *company?*

Who are *they?*

Where's Bill?

Model the three questions so you stress the *Wh-* question and nouns or pronouns. Drill the students and draw attention to the fact that normally we stress these words, but do not stress the verb *to be*, even when it is not a contraction.

Photocopiable worksheet

Download and photocopy *Unit 3 Language at work worksheet* from the teacher resources in the *Online practice*.

Practically speaking

Exercise 1

▶ **3.5** You could play the listening once and students listen and read the email and website addresses. Then play it again and they can repeat them.

Exercise 2

▶ **3.5** Students listen and match the words to the symbols. If you feel your students may have come across these terms before, they could try to give the answers before listening.

Answers
1 at
2 dash
3 underscore
4 dot

Exercise 3

▶ **3.6** Students listen to a short conversation which contains one email address from **1**.

Answer
4 d.roberts@fisons.co.uk

Exercise 4

▶ **3.7** Students listen again for a very useful phrase. Once you've elicited the answer, ask your students in which situations this phrase may be useful for them.

Answer
Can you repeat that?

Further practice

If students need more practice, go to *Practice file 3* on page 61 of the *Student's Book*.

Exercise 5

Students fill in the first column with their own details. If they don't have a company website or they don't want to use real details, they can make up the information or base it on a real company.

Exercise 6

Students can either dictate their information to each other or you could prompt them to ask questions using *What …?* For example, *What's your website? What's your work email?* Also encourage students to use the expression *Can you repeat that?* so they hear the details twice, as in the listening in **4**.

EXTENSION To extend the activity in **6** or to adapt it for pre-work learners, students could also dictate their home email or the address of their favourite website.

Business communication

Exercise 1

You might need to pre-teach the words *map* and *request* before starting this lesson. Show the students a map (either paper or online), explain that a request means 'asking for something', and model it by asking a student for something.

Note that students read two different emails, but they are both about a visit and they have the same request. When students are reading the emails to answer the questions, avoid letting them get stuck on all the language. They should focus on the key words at this stage.

Answers
1 to a new factory and warehouse
2 to ask for a map

EXTENSION You could ask the students to underline differences in the two emails. For example, the use of titles, surnames, and first names. Some phrases are different and one email is longer. At this stage, students don't need to talk about formal or informal writing (see **4**), but it's useful to notice basic differences before the next activity.

Exercise 2

Students should be able to match the emails because of the style and language use.

Answers
email 1 → email 4
email 2 → email 3

Exercise 3

Students complete the two lists of expressions. They can write the expressions in and check their answers by looking back at the four emails or at *Key expressions*.

Answers

Emails 1 and 4	Emails 2 and 3
Dear Ms Aranegui / Mr Galletti	**Hi** Maria / Hello Luca
I'm writing about my visit to your new factory …	**Where is** the new factory …?
Thank you for	Thanks for
Can you please send …	Please send
Please find attached	**Here is**
Best wishes / **Kind regards**	**All the best** / Best

Exercise 4

When students give the answer, ask them for reasons. For example, formal emails use *Dear + title + surname* and the expressions are longer.

Answer
Emails 1 and 4 are formal.

Further practice

If students need more practice, go to *Practice file 3* on page 60 of the *Student's Book*.

Exercise 5

Before the students start to complete the emails, as a class look at the two emails and discuss which is the formal email and how they know.

Answers
1 Hi / Hello
2 Please send
3 Dear
4 I am writing about
5 Best wishes / Kind regards

EXTRA ACTIVITY

Put students in pairs. Tell each student to write an email on their own to their partner requesting details about their next meeting. They can decide if the email is formal or less formal. Then they swap their emails. Now they write a reply to their partner. At the end, the students can read and compare their emails. Encourage students to help each other with any corrections.

Provide help while the students are writing their emails, but you can also collect the emails in at the end of the lesson to assess how much the students have learnt. It may also be the first opportunity you have had on the course to evaluate your students' writing ability.

Photocopiable worksheet

Download and photocopy *Unit 3 Business communication worksheet* from the teacher resources in the *Online practice*.

Talking point

Decide if students are to work in pairs or in teams. If the class is very mixed ability, it's useful for them to work in teams for this final activity. Student A / Team A looks at the squares at the top of the page and Student B / Team B looks at the squares at the bottom of the page.

Student A / Team A goes first and asks a question from a blue square. Student B / Team B must say a correct response from a yellow square. If both teams agree the response is correct, then Student B / Team B gets a point. If they can't agree, they ask you.

Answers

Is the factory in Russia?	Yes, it is.
Where are the offices?	They're in Dubai.
Are they in reception?	No, they're in the car park.
Where is Simon?	He's in the cafeteria.
Is the factory new or old?	It's old.
Where is the head office?	It's in Lima.
Is Claudia in the warehouse?	Yes, she is.
Is your office big?	Yes, it is.

EXTENSION To extend the activity, ask each student or team to prepare four more questions. They can look back through Units 1 to 3 for ideas. When they have four questions, they work with the other student or team again and ask their questions. The other student / team gets a point for a correct answer.

ONE-TO-ONE With one-to-one classes, you can either play the game with you taking part as Student B, or alternatively ask the student to read each question on the board aloud for Student A / Team A and to suggest a possible answer. Write the four answers down and then turn to the other board to compare their answers. Then repeat the process by looking at the questions on the other board and comparing with the answer on the board for Student A / Team A.

Progress test

Download and photocopy *Unit 3 Progress test* and *Speaking test* from the teacher resources in the *Online practice*.

4 Departments

Unit content

By the end of this unit, students will be able to

- talk about responsibilities and departments
- ask about people and departments
- describe departments
- take and leave a message on the phone.

Context

Having been introduced to language for giving basic personal details, talking about their jobs, and describing parts of their companies, this unit introduces students to the language they'll need to talk about working with other people, both in a department or as part of a team. *Working with words* also introduces the language they need to describe the basic details of their role at work. This language will be helpful when introducing themselves to business contacts for the first time.

So far, students have used the verb *to be* in its present simple form, but this is the first time that the tense is formally looked at in *Language at work* with the *I / you / we / they* forms. (Note that the *he / she / it* form is dealt with in the next unit.) The verbs used have already been presented in *Working with words*, so the main challenge for students will be to use the auxiliary *do / don't* in negatives, questions, and short answers. In addition, *Practically speaking* introduces *there is / there are* in its affirmative form so that students can talk about their company and how it is organized in more detail. By the end of this section, students will be in a position to give short but effective presentations of introduction.

In *Unit 2*, students learnt the basic phrases to start and end a phone call. Now they build on this language in *Business communication* by recycling the language and extending it to include expressions for taking and leaving phone messages. The unit also revises saying letters, emails, websites, and numbers from previous units so that, by the end, students will have developed a very useful phone skill.

In the *Talking point*, students practise listening to and taking notes on different voicemail messages, and discussing which department the voicemails are for.

Starting point

From previous lessons, you probably have a good idea of which department students work in or the type of team they are part of. Work through the questions as a class and introduce any necessary words to help students talk about their department. If you have students who don't work in a department, focus on question 3 and ask about whether they work in a team or on their own.

PRE-WORK LEARNERS If your students are at a college or university, write these alternative *Starting point* questions on the board for them to discuss:

What departments are in the university / college?

Which department are you in?

Working with words

Exercise 1

▶ **4.1** After students listen and read the two texts once, you could play the listening again and ask students to speak along with the person on the listening to practise saying the new words in the text.

Exercise 2

Students read the two texts and complete the table.

ALTERNATIVE With false beginners and stronger classes, you could make the activity into a listening task where students listen to the texts instead of reading them and fill in the table. Afterwards, let them read the texts to check their answers.

Answers

Name	Joanna	Fred Meesmaecker
Home	Hungary	England
Job	Sales rep	Project manager
What you do	Meet customers, sell the products	Manage a team
Number of people	Three	Eight

Exercise 3

Do the first two or three together as a class and then students underline the rest of the verbs. Note that the text includes forms of the verb *to be*, but it isn't necessary for students to underline these.

Answers

Text 1: live, work, make, meet, sell, have, work
Text 2: live, work, have, manage, have, manage, have

EXTENSION You could draw attention to the prepositions that often follow certain verbs by writing these on the board: *work for, live in*. With the other verbs, it might be helpful to note how the verbs *make* and *sell* are followed by words related to products (*make online products, sell the products*, etc.). The verbs *meet, have*, and *manage* are sometimes followed by words connected with people (*meet customers, have three people, manage a team of IT specialists*, etc.). This kind of analysis will help students to see patterns and to help them complete the next activity.

Exercise 4

Students complete the text with the verbs. Ask them to check with a partner before giving the answers as a class.

Answers

1 live
2 work
3 make
4 manage
5 have
6 meet
7 sell

Exercise 5

▶ **4.2** Play the listening and then check that everyone can say the verbs in **4**. In particular, check that they put the stress on the first syllable of the word *manage*.

Exercise 6

Students write a similar text about themselves, using the verbs in **4**. Encourage them to try and use all seven verbs if they can, though some might not be relevant. Afterwards, students read their texts to each other.

PRE-WORK LEARNERS To adapt the activity for pre-work learners, teach them the verb *study*. Then they can write a description with the verbs *live, study, meet, have*. Alternatively, they could make up a person with a job title and write about their fictional life.

Exercise 7

▶ **4.3** Allow time for students to study the company and the pictures of the six departments at work. Then students listen and repeat the departments.

PRONUNCIATION You could also ask students to listen and write the number of syllables and underline the stressed syllables in each department name (except, of course, IT).

Answers

Lo<u>gis</u>tics (3)   <u>Fin</u>ance (2)
<u>Sales</u> (1)   <u>Hu</u>man (2) Re<u>sour</u>ces (3)
Pro<u>duc</u>tion (3)

Exercise 8

This activity clarifies students' understanding of what each person and their department is responsible for in a company.

Answers

1 Carlos
2 Greta
3 Carl and Dan
4 Antony
5 Andreas
6 Ilse
7 Anne-Marie

EXTENSION Ask students to name some of the departments in their company. Then ask them to write one sentence about each department. The students can begin each sentence with *They*, e.g. *They make car parts*. (Avoid constructions beginning with *It …* or *The department …* because the third person form with -*s* is presented in *Unit 5*.)

Exercise 9

▶ **4.4** Students now know numbers 0–9, so it's easy to present the idea of plurals. Ask them to find the plural forms for all the words in the texts in **1**, **4** and **8**. Students can listen and check their answers.

Answers

departments	people
companies	products
employees	technicians
customers	countries
offices	

So that students understand the spelling rules behind plural forms, ask them to read the *Tip*. Note that none of the words on this page is followed by -es (e.g. *boxes*, *churches*). In particular, students should notice that some nouns can be irregular, and you could show them that a good dictionary indicates when a noun has an irregular plural form by asking them to look up the word *person*.

Also advise students to make a note of the plural form when they write down nouns in the future.

PRONUNCIATION When you play the listening for students to listen and repeat, you might want to draw attention to the fact that these -s endings can have three different sounds: /s/, /z/ and /ɪz/. These are shown in the answer key below in case you would like to focus on this area.

Answers

departments /s/	people
companies /z/	products /s/
employees /z/	technicians /z/
customers /z/	countries /z/
offices /ɪz/	

Further practice
If students need more practice, go to *Practice file 4* on page 62 of the *Student's Book*.

Exercise 10
Note that the activity limits the structure to six departments. Some students might want to draw the whole structure, but with very large companies, students should just choose part of the company, such as a division with a few departments. In some cases, it will be easier if the students simplify the structure in order to focus on practising the target language.

If possible, have students draw the structure on large pieces of paper or design it as a PowerPoint slide so that they have a visual aid. Then ask students to give short presentations to the class.

If some of your students work for the same company, they could work in a group and draw their company structure. If the whole class is from the same company, they can draw in groups and then compare their drawings to see if they agree.

In feedback, focus on correct use of the verbs and pronunciation of the names of the departments and any plural forms.

PRE-WORK LEARNERS Ask students to work in pairs or groups of three. Tell them to make up a company. They write its name and what it produces. Then they draw the structure for their imaginary company in the style of the company shown in **7**. If possible, have students draw the structure on large pieces of paper or design it as a PowerPoint slide so that they have a visual aid. Then ask students to give short presentations to the class.

Photocopiable worksheet
Download and photocopy *Unit 4 Working with words worksheet* from the teacher resources in the *Online practice*.

Language at work

Exercise 1
▶ 4.5 Students read the details and then listen to the beginning of the meeting.

Answers
Karla – Human Resources
Astrid – Sales
Mark – Finance

Exercise 2
▶ 4.5 Students could try to complete the sentences before listening if they are false beginners. Then they can listen and check.

Answers
1 manage
2 don't
3 live
4 work
5 do
6 do
7 work
8 don't

Exercise 3
You could begin by asking students to look back at the sentences in **2** and identify the affirmative sentences, negative sentences, questions, and short answers. Then ask them to complete the table in the *Language point* with *do* or *don't*.

Answers

Positive	Negative	Question	Short answers
I / you / we / they manage a department.	I / you / we / they **don't** work in Sales.	**Do** you / they live in Germany?	Yes, I / we / they **do**. No, I / we / they **don't**.

Grammar reference
If students need more information, go to *Grammar reference* on page 63 of the *Student's Book*.

Exercise 4
Note that there are more than six possible questions, so allow students to make different possibilities. Do one together to demonstrate what to do.

Possible answers
Do you manage a department / people / a team?
Do you live in Spain / India?
Do you work in a department / Spain / a team / India?
Do you meet people?
Do you sell products?
Do you make products?

EXTENSION Ask students if they can make more questions with the same verbs. Ideally they might relate to their specific business such as: *Do you manage a sales office? Do you live in Germany? Do you work in a factory?*

Exercise 5

Students work in pairs and ask and answer the questions in **4**. If you did the extension task above, students could add some of these questions as well.

PRE-WORK LEARNERS Ask students to choose a local or well-known company and imagine they work there.

Exercise 6

Students used these *Wh-* question words with the verb *to be* in the previous unit, so they should be familiar with them. Because students have already learnt the question *What's your job?* (see *Unit 1*), refer them to the *Tip* so they see that *What do you do?* has the same meaning.

Answers
1 What
2 Who
3 Where

PRONUNCIATION For additional pronunciation work, you can look at sentence stress in the question forms. Write the three questions from **6** on the board and underline the words as shown here:

What do you do?
Who do you work for?
Where do you live?

Model and drill the three questions so you stress the *Wh-* question and the main verb.

Exercise 7

Students read eight answers and make questions for each one.

Answers
What do you do?
I'm a production manager. / We manage training courses. / I make computers. / I'm an engineer. / I sell products.
Who do you work for?
We work for a small IT company. / I work for Alcatel-Lucent.
Where do you live?
We live in Lima.

EXTENSION Working in their pairs from **7**, students can ask each other the three questions before the final task.

Further practice

If students need more practice, go to *Practice file 4* on page 63 of the *Student's Book*.

Exercise 8

The whole class stands and walks around and students ask each other the three questions. If the class is too large, put students into smaller groups of five or six.

As students do **8**, you can join in the activity in order to listen to individual students and give help where necessary. Anticipate that some students will have difficulty with the auxiliary *do* and word order in their questions.

ONE-TO-ONE Download and cut up the *Business cards* from the teacher resources in the *Online practice*. Both you and your student can select a card and ask the questions, then take another card and assume a different identity each time.

Photocopiable worksheet

Download and photocopy *Unit 4 Language at work worksheet* from the teacher resources in the *Online practice*.

Practically speaking

Exercise 1

We use *there is ('s)* / *there are* to say that something exists, but at this level avoid any description like this. Present the structure through the context of the sentences in **1**. Once students have underlined the verbs, draw attention to the fact that *there are* is used with plurals and *there's* with singular nouns.

> **Answers**
> There <u>are</u> four people in my department. There<u>'s</u> a manager at head office. There <u>are</u> two IT technicians and there<u>'s</u> an assistant.

Exercise 2

Students compare the sentences and complete with *is ('s)* or *are*.

> **Answers**
> 's / is
> are

PRONUNCIATION Make sure students are saying the contraction *there's*. You could also drill the pronunciation of *there are* and draw students' attention to the linking /r/ sound that occurs like this: there /r/ are.

Exercise 3

Students can work in pairs and practise reading the sentences aloud after they have completed them.

> **Answers**
> 1 are
> 2 's
> 3 are
> 4 's

> **Further practice**
> If students need more practice, go to *Practice file 4* on page 63 of the *Student's Book*.

Exercise 4

Allow students some time to prepare their sentences with *there is* / *there are*. You could allow them to write the sentences in full before speaking. If you have students from the same company, they could work together on their sentences and give a small presentation to the class.

PRE-WORK LEARNERS As an alternative, students at universities or colleges could write sentences about a company they know well, or they could write about their place of study, including:

- the number of classrooms
- different departments
- the number of teachers and/or lecturers

Business communication

Exercise 1

These lead-in questions introduce the context of making calls internally around the office and that many companies use English as their company language. Discuss both questions as a class. Miss the questions out with pre-work learners and go straight to **2**.

Exercise 2

▶ 4.6 Before students start listening, you could ask them to read the message and say what type of information is missing; for example name of a department, type of website, end of a web address and a phone number.

> **Answers**
> 1 IT
> 2 sales
> 3 .co.uk?
> 4 07700 897 833

Exercise 3

▶ 4.6 Play the listening again and students complete the conversation. Refer them to the *Key expressions* on the left of the page for help, or to check their answers.

> **Answers**
> 1 a message
> 2 I'm calling
> 3 Go ahead
> 4 don't
> 5 repeat
> 6 Is there
> 7 call, back
> 8 give, message

Exercise 4

Students play the parts of Martha and Janusz and read the conversation in **3**.

EXTENSION Ask students to cover the conversation in **3** and role-play the phone call again, but only using the notes in the message in **2**. They don't have to use exactly the same words, but they should try to follow the same structure, and they can use phrases from *Key expressions*.

PRONUNCIATION Students should try to use friendly and polite intonation on the phone, so you could drill some of the expressions in *Key expressions* if you feel students need to (or are ready to) work on this area.

> **Further practice**
> If students need more practice, go to *Practice file 4* on page 62 of the *Student's Book*.

Exercise 5

Students turn to the pages indicated and role-play two phone conversations, so sit them back to back or use real phones. After they have done both role-plays, give feedback and then ask them to change partners and repeat the activities if necessary.

Taking and leaving a message brings together a number of language points, including some from previous units such as spelling, saying numbers and saying websites, as well as the new language on the page. Provide remedial help with any recurring errors.

> **EXTRA ACTIVITY**
> Ask each student to prepare a message for a real person they work with in their own company. Then they work in pairs and take turns to phone and leave the message for the person in their workplace.

Photocopiable worksheet

Download and photocopy *Unit 4 Business communication worksheet* from the teacher resources in the *Online practice*.

Talking point

Unlike *Units 1* to *3*, this *Talking point* is more like a case study, so you will need to lead students through it carefully, step by step. The basic scenario is that the students work at the head office of a company called Synox Solutions and they receive three voicemails. They have to note the key information and then decide which person on the company contacts list needs to receive the message.

Exercise 1

Students read about the company and answer the questions.

> **Answers**
> 1 in Bristol in England
> 2 They manage computer systems and write new software.
> 3 Human Resources and Sales. The rest of the staff are IT technicians and they work in teams (not departments).
> 4 This last question is subjective and what students answer may depend on the size of their own company. However, from the description it sounds like quite a large independent company.

Exercise 2

▶ **4.7** Students may need to listen twice to make sure they have the key information. Make sure they aren't trying to write every word, but that they listen for the main words only. After each message, students can compare their answers with a partner.

> **Suggested answers**
> **Message 1**
> Caller: Raul Avasthi
> Reason for call: A software problem in the office in Dubai
> Message: Call 00941 775 7568
> **Message 2**
> Caller: Emily in HR
> Reason for call: Problem with car
> Message: Tell her team she's late
> **Message 3**
> Caller: Jan Wilders in Rotterdam
> Reason for call: Problem with new software
> Message: Call him on his mobile: 0031 476 4857. It's very urgent!

Exercise 3

Students work together and talk about which person on the list of names and departments needs to deal with the message. To complete the task, students need to think about the departments and what they are responsible for.

> **Answers**
> Message 1 is for Tyler Khan-Yates because this is a caller from Dubai. Tyler deals with the Middle East region so he should call first.
> Message 2 is for Gill Reeves because she is Emily's assistant in HR.
> Message 3 is from an existing customer so can probably go to Frank Rogers in IT Projects or to his assistant, Ray Searle-Jones.

Exercise 4

The students should present their answers to the class and give their reasons.

Progress test

Download and photocopy *Unit 4 Progress test* and *Speaking test* from the teacher resources in the *Online practice*.

Viewpoint 1

Preview

The topic of this *Viewpoint* is *People in business*. It recycles a lot of vocabulary from *Units 1–4* in the context of real interviews with business people. In this *Viewpoint*, students begin by watching videos of six people answering basic questions about their names, countries, cities, companies and the location of their head office. Students write down key information and then practise similar question and answer conversations in pairs. Students then watch three more people, who work for different companies. They talk about the department they work in and their daily responsibilities. Finally, students practise the questions from the lesson and then prepare and deliver a short presentation about their own working life.

Exercise 1

Allow students time to look at the words and order them correctly. Students can also compare their questions with a partner.

Exercise 2

▶ 01 Play the video for students to check their answers in **1**. If necessary, pause the video after each question to check understanding.

Answers
1 What's your name?
2 Where are you from?
3 What is your company?
4 Where's your head office?

VIDEO SCRIPT

My name is Tina.
I'm from Los Angeles.
My company's name is Pepper Hamilton.
Our head office is in Philadelphia, Pennsylvania.

My name is Vikram.
I'm from India.
I work for Lloyds TSB.
In London.

My name is Christine.
I'm from Hong Kong.
My company is HSBC.
My head office is in London.

Exercise 3

▶ 01 Before you play the video again, give the students time to study the table and understand what type of language they need to write in. They might even remember some of the answers from their first viewing, so they could try and complete some of the table before watching again.

Play the video and ask students to complete the notes in the table. Afterwards, let them compare their answers before checking together as a class. If necessary, play the video again, pausing after each speaker for students to check the answers.

Answers
1 Los Angeles
2 India
3 London
4 HSBC
5 London

Exercise 4

The sentences given in this exercise refer to new people who will appear in the next part of the video. Students should be able to complete the missing words, which were already introduced in *Units 1–4*. If you notice that students are finding the exercise difficult, allow them to work in pairs or small groups and help each other, or you could play the video now rather than waiting until **5**.

Exercise 5

▶ 02 Play the video for students to check their answers in **4**.

Answers
1 name
2 from
3 in
4 My
5 I'm
6 for
7 is
8 is
9 in
10 company

VIDEO SCRIPT

My name's Ulric Bogaerde.
I'm from London.
Blackwells, the bookshop.
It's in Oxford.

My name is Naomi.
I'm from New Zealand.
I work for a publishing company.
My head office is in Oxford.

My name is Charles.
I'm from Aberdeen, in Scotland.
My company is called ETPM.
In Aberdeen.

PRONUNCIATION Check students' pronunciation of the questions in **1** and the phrases in **4**. In particular, drill the contracted forms including *what's*, *where's*, *name's*, *it's*, and *I'm*.

Exercise 6

Student B needs to choose a person in the video and use the information provided in the table in **3** or the sentences in **4**. They will need some time to prepare answers to the questions in **1**, which Student A will ask them. When they are ready, Student A asks his/her questions. Monitor the conversations closely and give feedback, with the main focus on correct question forms and the use of the verb *to be*.

Exercise 7

Students swap roles and repeat the activity from **6**.

ALTERNATIVE You could ask the students to record themselves using the voice recorder or video on their phones. Then they can play back their conversations and listen out for what they did well and any mistakes they made.

Exercise 8

▶ 03 In this next video, students hear longer answers to the questions and will have to listen more carefully. Before watching, they should read the seven true / false sentences and underline any content words they will need to listen out for, such as *training manager* and *Human Resources Department*. Once they have underlined the content words, you could also check that they remember what they mean; they have already been taught the meanings in *Units 1–4*, so this is a good opportunity for revision.

Now play the video and the students decide if the sentences are true (*T*) or false (*F*). Note that the three people speak twice and sentences 1–7 in the book are listed chronologically. Check answers with the whole class.

Answers
1 T
2 F (She's from the USA, but she lives in London.)
3 F (She works in the IT department of an insurance company.)
4 T
5 T
6 T
7 F (He's never in his office His office is his car or a café.)

VIDEO SCRIPT

E My name's Emma Sanders. I'm a training manager. I'm from the USA, but I live in London. I work for a large insurance company.

K I'm Kate Roberts. I'm from London. I work in the IT Department of an insurance company.

A My name is Alex Mitchell. I work for a training company. I'm in the Sales Department. I'm a sales rep.

E My department is the Human Resources Department. I manage the training for the employees here. We have ten people in the HR Department, and three in the training team. We do training courses for all the departments – Sales, Marketing, and Finance. We run a lot of training courses – training for presentations, communication skills, languages, IT, finance, everything. People need training all the time.

K My company has six departments – Sales, Marketing, Finance, Human Resources, Business Development, and IT. I like my department. I work with eleven IT technicians in one big office. We manage the computer systems here, and we work with all of the departments. We fix computers and we make new programmes for the company systems. It's very interesting.

A We make online training programmes. I sell the programmes to companies. I travel around the country and present the training programmes to HR and training managers. I meet four or five new people every day. We have four reps in the Sales Department, but I don't see them because I'm never in the office. My office is my car. Or a café!

Exercise 9

All nine sentences are from the video and students will have met most of the verbs. They may have to guess others from context. Allow the use of dictionaries where necessary. Check answers with the whole class.

Answers
1 manage
2 have
3 run
4 like
5 work
6 fix, make
7 sell
8 travel
9 meet

EXTRA ACTIVITY
For further practice, ask students to choose five of the verbs and write sentences about their own job or – if they are pre-work students – they could choose five verbs and write about their place of study and daily life. Then ask the students to read their sentences aloud to a partner. Check the use of the verbs.

Exercise 10

▶ 03 Before playing the video again, check students can say the names of the seven departments listed. Tell students to tick all the departments and teams each speaker mentions. Play the video. Check answers with the whole class.

Answers

	Emma	Kate	Alex
IT	✓	✓	
Sales	✓	✓	✓
Human Resources	✓	✓	✓
Marketing	✓	✓	
Finance	✓	✓	
Business Development		✓	
Training	✓		✓

Exercise 11

This exercise checks that students know how to use different question words and how to form basic questions.

Answers
1 Who
2 What
3 Where
4 What
5 How

Exercise 12

Students work on their own and prepare three new questions to ask their partner. Encourage them to look back through *Units 1–4* of the *Student's Book* for ideas, including the use of *Yes / No* questions such as *Are you …?*, *Is there …?*, *Do you …?*

PRE-WORK LEARNERS For pre-work students, write a similar exercise to **11** on the board or on a worksheet, such as the one below, and get the students to complete the sentences:

who what how where

1 _____ is your place of study?

2 _____ is your school / college / university?

3 _____ subjects do you study?

4 _____ is your teacher?

5 _____ many students are in your school / college / university?

Answers
1 What
2 Where
3 What
4 Who
5 How

Exercise 13

Put students into pairs and they take turns to ask their questions from **12**.

Exercise 14

In the previous exercises, the students have practised asking short questions and giving short answers. In this exercise, the focus shifts to students giving extended information about their working life. If you have run out of classroom time, then set this exercise for homework if necessary. Students might want to write out sentences about their job to help them, or they could practise the presentation by recording themselves. As students work on the presentations, go around to each student and provide any extra vocabulary they need which is specific to their own job.

PRE-WORK LEARNERS Ask the students to think about and present the following:

- your name and where you live
- your school / college / university
- your department or types of subjects
- your subject and what you do

Exercise 15

Students work with new partners and give their presentations from **14**. If the class is a small group of students and you feel that they have bonded well, then you could have students take turns to give their presentation to everyone. Remember that low-level learners will need lots of praise if they manage to give a presentation to a group of people, and encourage the rest of the group to listen and give positive feedback, too.

Further video ideas

You can find a list of suggested ideas for how to use video in the class in the teacher resources in the *Online practice*.

5 Products

Starting point

This first question reviews the verbs *make* and *sell* which were taught in *Unit 4*. If you think your students may for some reason not know the name Microsoft, then you could ask them the same question, but choose a company from their own locality. Even if you do ask them about Microsoft, you could still ask them the same question in 1, but about some other local companies. For questions 2 and 3, students need to personalize their answers. Note that these questions use the third person form. If students ask about the *does* auxiliary, explain that it is similar to the *do* form and that they will look at it later. At this stage, students only need to give one-word answers in response to the questions. They will have the opportunity to use the third person in fuller answers later in the unit.

PRE-WORK LEARNERS Students can talk about a local company or a company a friend or family member works for.

Working with words

Exercise 1

▶ **5.1** Students look at the five photos and match them to the company names in the list. Then students listen to three sentences for each picture. The first two sentences include the name of the company and the company type. The aim is that students hear these words and recognize what type of company each one is from the picture.

Answers
1 Gazprom
2 Dassault
3 Aldi
4 Toyota
5 Samsung

Exercise 2

▶ **5.1** If students seem familiar with the companies in the listening, they could match the products first and then listen to check.

Answers

	Company type	Products
Gazprom	energy	oil and gas
Dessault	aeronautical	aeroplanes
Aldi	retail	food
Toyota	automobile	cars
Samsung	electronics	televisions and mobiles

PRONUNCIATION Read the list of company types aloud to students and ask them to underline the stressed syllable, like this: _energy_, _aeronautical_, _retail_, _automobile_, _electronics_. Then ask students to practise saying them with the correct stress.

EXTENSION Ask students to think of and say three more companies, perhaps from their own countries, that are similar company types to three in the table in **2** and that make three of the same products. This is a useful way to check their understanding and pronunciation of the vocabulary presented so far.

EXTRA ACTIVITY
For consolidation of the new language presented in **1** and **2**, you could ask students to turn to page 77 and read the audio script as they listen, or they could practise reading the sentences aloud.

Exercise 3

Student A needs to imagine that he/she works for one of the five companies and says which one (e.g. _I work for Aldi_). Then Student B asks the questions. Afterwards, the students can swap roles and choose another company.

EXTENSION Students can follow on from **3** by asking and answering questions about their own companies with similar conversations.

Exercise 4

▶ **5.2** Students listen and read the text and then answer the questions about Embraer and Uniqlo. The exact words don't appear in the text, so they need to use the whole text and picture to guess the correct company type.

Answers
Embraer is an aeronautical company.
Uniqlo is a retail company.

EXTENSION You can extend the reading task by asking students to find information in each text about the two companies. You could draw this table on the board and ask students to complete it with words from the text. (Answers shown in brackets in table.)

	Embraer	Uniqlo
Nationality	(Brazilian)	(Japanese)
Product	(aeroplanes)	(clothes)
Location of factories or stores	(in Brazil)	(in 13 countries)
Exports and online sales	(exports to China, USA, and Europe)	(has an online store)

EXTRA ACTIVITY
This is a good moment to refer students to the _Tip_ because they have read the two nationalities, _Brazilian_ and _Japanese_, in the text. Write these two sentences on the board:

Embraer is a Brazilian company.
They have factories in Brazil.

Draw attention to the adjective (_Brazilian_) and the noun (_Brazil_). Next, students study the list of countries and nationalities in the _Tip_. You can say the words aloud and students can listen and repeat.

Also ask them to make two sentences about their own company (or place of study) similar to those on the board. You will need to provide the countries and nationalities for the students in the class if they are not included in the _Tip_.

Exercise 5

Students match the verbs in the list to the pictures. If necessary, ask students to look back at the two texts and find the verbs in the list. Note that the answers are given in **6**.

Exercise 6

▶ **5.3** Let students listen and check their answers before they listen again and practise saying them.

Answers
1 buy
2 export
3 design
4 deliver
5 build
6 order

Exercise 7

Students underline the verbs to check their understanding.

Answers
1 build
2 design
3 buy
4 order
5 deliver

Further practice
If students need more practice, go to *Practice file 5* on page 64 of the *Student's Book*.

Exercise 8

Students can either write the sentences on their own, or if they work for the same company, they could work in pairs.

Exercise 9

If you have time, students could prepare PowerPoint slides to illustrate different aspects of their company. Encourage them to use photographs and include key facts.

Some students may find presenting their sentences to the whole class quite a challenge, so give lots of praise for their efforts. Make sure they use the correct verbs and help with any word stress difficulties that affect intelligibility.

PRE-WORK LEARNERS For **8** and **9**, students could choose a company they know well or one that they would like to research. If they have time, they could also prepare PowerPoint slides and give a formal presentation with the key facts.

Photocopiable worksheet
Download and photocopy *Unit 5 Working with words worksheet* from the teacher resources in the *Online practice*.

Language at work

Exercise 1

▶ 5.4 The two texts that students read and listen to are similar to those on the previous page in terms of content. However, in these texts students see verbs in the present simple with the third person -s for the first time, so it's useful for them to listen and hear the pronunciation of the verbs in particular.

Exercise 2

Students read the texts again and complete the table.

ALTERNATIVE Students cover the texts and listen only. They write the missing information down as they listen.

Answers

	Type of company	Products
Auchan	Retail	food and clothes
LG	Electronics	televisions and mobile phones

Exercise 3

As students underline the verbs, ask them if the subject of the sentence is a person (*he / she*) or a company (*it*).

Answers
Auchan: is, sells, has, is, works, doesn't work, is
LG: is, makes, sells, works, designs, has, exports

Exercise 4

Students study the verbs and complete the grammar table in the *Language point*. Note that examples of questions or short answers are not provided in the text, so if students are having difficulty, remind them that in the last unit they started questions with *Do ...?* and ended short answers with *do* and *don't*. Explain that they need to use *does / doesn't* in the same way with *he / she / it*.

Answers

Positive	Negative	Question	Short answers
He / she / it sell**s** food products.	He / she / it **doesn't** design new products.	**Does** he / she / it make products?	Yes, he / she / it **does**. No, he / she / it **doesn't**.

Use this opportunity in class to draw attention to the auxiliary verb and the main verb in negatives and questions. Ask students which verb changes its form. The aim is that students recognize how the third person -s is added to the auxiliary *do* and not to the main verb.

Draw students' attention to the *Tip* and the use of the verb *have* in the two texts. Logically, the third person form should be *haves*, but it is an irregular verb and we say *has*.

PRONUNCIATION In *Unit 4*, students were introduced to plural nouns, and you might have worked on the pronunciation of the -s at the end of the nouns. If so, students might also notice how the sound of third person -s changes at the end of the verbs. Otherwise, you could introduce the change now. Present the two phonemes /s/ and /z/ on the board. Then read these verbs and ask students to decide if they end with a /s/ or /z/ sound: *sells* /z/, *has* /z/, *works* /s/, *does* /z/, *makes* /s/, *designs* /z/, *exports* /s/. Afterwards, students can practise the pronunciation in pairs.

Grammar reference

If students need more information, go to *Grammar reference* on page 65 of the *Student's Book*.

Exercise 5

Students check their understanding of the rule for the positive and negative forms by completing the sentences. If you focused on the pronunciation issue of /s/ and /z/, ask students to practise reading the sentences aloud with the correct pronunciation of the verbs ending in -*s*.

Answers
1 sells
2 doesn't work
3 has
4 designs
5 exports
6 doesn't make

Exercise 6

Students can refer to the word order shown in the table in **4** to complete these questions.

Answers
1 Does Martin work in Croix?
2 Does LG export products?
3 Does Auchan have stores in Africa?
4 Does Soo Jin Lee design new products?
5 Does she work in the Sales Department?

Exercise 7

Note that the six questions in **6** all refer back to the two texts in **1**, so students can read these again in order to match the answers. Note that the answers are given as part of **8**.

Exercise 8

▶ 5.5 Play the listening so students can check their answers.

Answers
a 3
b 4
c 1
d 2
e 5

EXTENSION Play the listening again and ask students to listen and repeat the questions and answers. Then put them into pairs and ask them to practise asking and answering the five questions.

Exercise 9

So far, students have practised asking *Yes / No* questions with *Does …?* However, they already know three *Wh-* question words and how to construct a question with them. So this activity is a quick review, but this time with the third person auxiliary *does*.

Answers
1 Where
2 Who
3 What

EXTENSION As a follow-up to the three questions, ask students to say the answers:

Answers
1 Martin works in Calais.
2 Soo Jin works for LG.
3 LG exports televisions and mobile phones.

Exercise 10

Students can match the questions to the answers on their own, and then work with a partner to check their answers and say them aloud.

Answers
1 b
2 e
3 a
4 c
5 d

Further practice

If students need more practice, go to *Practice file 5* on page 65 of the *Student's Book*.

Exercise 11

Students turn to the pages indicated. They have information on one company and need to ask questions about the other company. If you think some students might have difficulty forming questions to ask about a company, put them in pairs with another student, so two Student As work together and two Student Bs work together to prepare the questions together. Then switch the pairs so an A and a B are working together to complete the task.

Students will need plenty of time to complete the final task. Monitor carefully and be ready to help with non-use or over-use of the third person -*s*. Make a note of any recurring mistakes, and deal with them afterwards by presenting them to the class and asking them to spot the mistake.

EXTENSION Ask students to work in pairs and prepare *Does* and *Wh-* questions for each other about their companies and products.

Photocopiable worksheet

Download and photocopy *Unit 5 Language at work worksheet* from the teacher resources in the *Online practice*.

Practically speaking

Exercise 1

▶ **5.6** Begin this part of the lesson by checking that students remember how to say numbers 0–9. Then play the listening. Afterwards you could go round the class and ask students to count from 10 to 100.

Exercise 2

Students dictate their six numbers to each other. For further practice, students can swap partners and repeat the activity.

Exercise 3

▶ **5.7** Students listen and repeat larger numbers.

If some of your students are likely to communicate with American English speakers in the future, you could point out that they will say a number such as 145 without the *and* in the middle, like this: *one hundred forty-five*.

Exercise 4

▶ **5.8** Students listen and write the numbers.

> **Answers**
> 1 1,660
> 2 250
> 3 424,000,000
> 4 59, 14

> | **Further practice**
> If students need more practice, go to *Practice file 5* on page 65 of the *Student's Book*.

Exercise 5

Students make sentences about the number of employees and the population. You could also ask them to make sentences about:

- the number of products their company makes / exports
- the number of stores / factories / warehouses it has.

PRE-WORK LEARNERS Ask students at universities or colleges to make sentences about a company they know well, or about their country. They could also describe their place of study; for example, the number of students and teachers it has, or the number of subjects it offers.

Business communication

Before starting, it might be helpful to clarify the meaning of the verb *order*. You can do this by asking a student *What does your company produce and sell?* and *Do you deliver the products?* Write the answers on the board. Then ask *Who are your customers?* and write the answer. Then write a full sentence: *[The name of the customer] orders [the name of the products] from [the name of the student's company]*. Ask other students to make similar sentences with the verb *order* about their companies and their customers.

Exercise 1

Students read about a packing company to set the context for this page.

> **Answer**
> Euroboxes sells cardboard boxes and packaging. Yes, it delivers the products.

Exercise 2

▶ **5.9** Give students time to study the order form before listening to the phone call. Find out if it's similar to order forms in their businesses. Clarify any vocabulary used in the columns, for example, the *item number* is the number you often see in catalogues next to the products.

> **Answers**
> 1 SSW-3411
> 2 10,000
> 3 2,000
> 4 SSW-3412
> 5 25
> 6 1,250
> 7 3,250

Exercise 3

Students can work in pairs and decide who says the expressions in 1–10. Answers are given as part of **4**.

Draw attention to the use of *I would (I'd) like / I want* in the expressions. They have the same meaning, but *would like* is more polite.

Exercise 4

▶ **5.9** Play the listening again so students can listen and check answers.

> **Answers**
> 1 Company
> 2 Customer
> 3 Company
> 4 Company
> 5 Customer
> 6 Customer
> 7 Customer
> 8 Company
> 9 Customer
> 10 Company

> | **Further practice**
> If students need more practice, go to *Practice file 5* on page 64 of the *Student's Book*.

Exercise 5

Students put the words into the correct order. Encourage them not to look at the *Key expressions* until they have completed the exercise. They could check their own answers once they have finished by reading the *Key expressions*.

Answers
1 Can I help you?
2 I'd like to order …
3 What's the price?
4 Does that include delivery?
5 Can you confirm my order by email?

Exercise 6

Students need time to prepare what they plan to say, so refer them to the *Key expressions*. With weaker classes, students could work in pairs first and write the conversation out in full. Once they have done the role-play, ask them to swap roles and try it again.

Focus on the correct use of the *Key expressions* and how the students say the numbers and letters when talking about item numbers, prices, and quantities. If necessary, drill any difficult language and repeat the role-plays. You could also work on the intonation used in the phone conversation to make it sound friendly and polite.

ONE-TO-ONE If your student deals with orders, ask them to bring in an example of an order form from their own company. Use this order form as the basis for a role-play situation in which the student takes the order and you play the part of a customer.

Photocopiable worksheet

Download and photocopy *Unit 5 Business communication worksheet* from the teacher resources in the *Online practice*.

Talking point

This game not only reviews all the question forms in this unit, but also revises all the forms from previous units. Students work in pairs and take turns to ask each other four questions on three different topics. The student who is answering also has the job of scoring the questions asked, using the tick boxes in the table. If one student thinks there is a mistake with the question, they can point this out or ask you to help them decide.

To help manage this activity, encourage the students not to read all numbered tasks at the beginning, but rather just number one, then number two, and so on. Make sure that they only ask questions about topic 1, and change roles before moving on to topic 2.

Note that the activity can take up to half an hour or more in total.

EXTENSION If you have time, end the lesson with all the students standing and walking around the classroom asking different people different questions from the list. They don't need to record the points, but the aim is for them to try and use any of the questions listed for further practice.

Progress test

Download and photocopy *Unit 5 Progress test* and *Speaking test* from the teacher resources in the *Online practice*.

6 Entertaining

Unit content

By the end of this unit, students will be able to

- talk about food and drinks
- talk about ability
- say days and times
- invite, accept and decline.

Context

In this unit, students talk about topics related to social English and their own free-time activities. It includes useful language for situations such as ordering food and drinks, and eating out with colleagues and clients. They also learn lots of words and expressions that will help with small talk and making invitations.

In *Working with words*, they learn lots of food vocabulary in the context of ordering from a menu in a company cafeteria. In the same context, students are introduced to expressions they need to ask for food, and for talking about likes and dislikes in relation to the types of food they prefer. *Language at work* presents *can / can't* for talking about ability in the context of how people spend their free time. Students have the chance to talk about topics other than work and to ask each other about their interests.

Practically speaking introduces the language of days and times so that students can talk about daily routines. Then they re-use this new vocabulary in *Business communication* because they practise the language for inviting people, which includes discussing times and days for going out with another person.

The *Talking point* ends the unit with a game which recycles all the language from the different pages of the unit and also revisits social expressions from previous units, such as introducing yourself and saying goodbye.

Starting point

This first question is quite culture-specific and might generate interesting responses. People in some countries often eat at their desk and continue to work, for example in the UK. However, in a country such as Italy, many workers tend to take a proper break for lunch and sit and have a meal. If you have a mixed-nationality class, compare the responses. Or ask students to comment on their experience of eating with colleagues overseas. The second question is a way to elicit any basic words connected with the topic of food. If students don't know any words for food in English, ask them to use their own language. Some food words, such as *pizza*, *pasta*, *sushi*, *burger*, *dahl*, and *satay*, are used internationally.

PRE-WORK LEARNERS For question 1, students can say where they normally eat lunch while at their place of study. For example, do they eat in a café, in the college cafeteria, or while they study? You could also teach them *packed lunch* and ask how many bring a packed lunch.

Working with words

Exercise 1

Students read the menu and begin by matching the items listed. Note that they are matching the whole dish, not just single food items. You might also need to clarify certain items, such as *vegetarian dishes*. Note that the answers are given in **2**.

Exercise 2

▶ **6.1** Students listen and check. Then play the listening again and they can listen and repeat.

In the next listening, the speakers talk about prices on the menu, so you could look at the *Tip* on page 36 before moving on. Read out the three ways of saying the prices in the *Tip*. Then put students in pairs and ask them to practise saying the prices for each dish on the menu. As the prices are in dollars and cents, you could also ask them to say the prices but using different currencies, so instead of saying *seven dollars fifty* for steak and fries, they can say *seven euros fifty* or *seven pounds fifty*.

Answers
1 steak and fries
2 mineral water
3 tea
4 chicken curry and rice
5 ice cream
6 cheese sandwich
7 orange juice
8 coffee
9 tomato soup with bread
10 salad
11 vegetable lasagne
12 chocolate cake

EXTENSION Ask students to say if they eat any of the dishes in the pictures for lunch or dinner in their country. They could also talk about and add other types of meat dishes, vegetarian dishes, desserts, and drinks. You could also ask the class to create their own international menu in English by listing their favourite dishes on the board with imaginary prices. (Note that this menu can be re-used in the suggested *Extension* activity after **6** in this section.)

Exercise 3

▶ **6.2** As a variation to the listening activity, ask students to listen once and say how many people are in the listening. (There are three, including the person who works in the cafeteria.) Then play it again and students decide if the sentences are true or false.

Answers
1 T
2 F (tomato soup with bread)
3 T
4 F (mineral water and tea)
5 T

Exercise 4

▶ **6.2** Students can either listen first or they could order the sentences and then listen to check. For more of a challenge, ask them also to note who says each sentence (answers in brackets).

Answers
a 2 (Jarvis)
b 3 (Shimura)
c 1 (cafeteria assistant)
d 5 (cafeteria assistant)
e 4 (Jarvis)

EXTENSION Refer students to the *Tip* to clarify the difference between *I'd like* and *I like*. Note that the pronunciation can sometimes cause difficulty between these two items. A simple activity is to read out six sentences with *I'd like* and *I like* and students have to identify which they hear. For example, read these sentences and students say which they hear:

I like steak.	*I like Indian food.*
I'd like sushi.	*I'd like Thai food.*
I'd like pizza.	*I like tea.*

Exercise 5

▶ **6.3** Students listen and repeat the sentences in **4**. Make sure their pronunciation is using polite intonation and the contracted forms *I'd* and *That's*. Also, if students ask for an explanation of *I'd like …*, explain that this construction also appeared in *Business communication* in *Unit 5* and it means the same as *I want*, but is the polite form.

Exercise 6

To set up this role-play, you could model the conversation with two students in the class before asking everyone to do it. After students finish one role-play, they can switch roles and repeat the conversation, but taking a different part each time. The role-plays will work better if the students are standing and the cafeteria assistant is behind a table as if it's the counter in a cafeteria.

Give feedback on correct use of the phrases in **4**, pronunciation of food words, and on saying prices.

EXTENSION In the *Extension* activity suggested after **2**, students brainstormed a menu as a class to write on the board. If you did this, ask students to try another conversation in a cafeteria, but this time they should refer to the items on the menu they created.

ONE-TO-ONE With one student, you will need to play two roles while the student plays one.

Exercise 7

▶ **6.4** The next conversation takes place between Mr Shimura and Mr Jarvis only. It is during their meal and provides students with a model of a conversation they might typically have over lunch. It also introduces them to the verb *to like* for the first time. The sentences use the verb in the present simple, so it recycles the grammar they learnt in *Units 4* and *5*.

Answers
1 Mr Shimura
2 Mr Shimura
3 Mr Jarvis
4 Mr Jarvis
5 Mr Shimura

Further practice

If students need more practice, go to *Practice file 6* on page 66 of the *Student's Book*.

Exercise 8

This is a discussion activity, in which students give authentic responses to the questions. With large classes, students work in groups, but with a smaller class, everyone can discuss the questions together. Note that nationality words were introduced in *Unit 5*, so this is a good chance to review that language by asking students about all sorts of other types of food, such as French food, Mexican food, Chinese food, etc. It is also a useful review of present simple questions and short answers with *do / don't*.

Photocopiable worksheet

Download and photocopy *Unit 6 Working with words worksheet* from the teacher resources in the *Online practice*.

Language at work

Exercise 1

The lead-in question follows the theme of the opening question in *Starting point* on the previous page and asks students about free time at lunchtime. Some students might reply *I don't have free time at lunchtime*, but others might work for companies where there are activities. If students don't know the word for what they do at lunchtime, you can translate it for them or ask them to mime the action and provide the word.

PRE-WORK LEARNERS   Students at university or college might also do sports or be in clubs or societies, so find out what they do in their free time between their lessons and studies.

Exercise 2

Students read about a real company in Wales where employees can sing in a choir at lunchtime. Most of the words in the text have appeared in previous units, and to teach the words *sing* and *choir*, refer students to the picture.

> **Answer**
> The employees meet and sing in a choir at lunchtime.

Exercise 3

▶ **6.5** The short conversation follows on from the context in the reading.

> **Answer**
> the woman

Exercise 4

▶ **6.5** Play the listening again and students complete the conversation in the *Language point*.

> **Answers**
> 1 Can
> 2 can
> 3 can't

Grammar reference

If students need more information, go to *Grammar reference* on page 67 of the *Student's Book*.

EXTENSION   In previous units, the *Language point* sections included a *Grammar reference* table for students to complete. Because the form of *can / can't* doesn't change, it isn't included here. However, if you feel your students would like more clarification of the structure, they can either turn to *Grammar reference* in the *Unit 6 Practice file* on page 67 of the *Student's Book* or you can draw this table on the board. Ask them to complete the missing parts of the table with *can* or *can't*.

Positive	Negative	Question	Short answers
I _____ sing. He can sing	I can't sing. She _____ sing.	_____ you sing?	Yes, I can. No, I _____.

PRONUNCIATION Read the sentences in **4** with *can / can't* aloud for students so they hear that the *a* in *can* has a short /æ/ sound and the *a* in *can't* has a longer /ɑː/ sound.

Exercise 5

Students practise the conversation in pairs. If you have worked on the pronunciation of /æ/ and /ɑː/ (see above), give feedback on their pronunciation and remedial help where necessary.

Exercise 6

▶ 6.6 Students listen and repeat the verb + noun collocations.

EXTRA ACTIVITY
If you have an outgoing class, ask a student to come to the front of the class and mime an activity in **6**. The other students guess the action. Then another student mimes another activity until the rest of the class guess the words.

Exercise 7

Students use the *can / can't* verb in combination with the verbs in **6**. They follow the structure provided in the example for each activity.

Further practice
If students need more practice, go to *Practice file 6* on page 67 of the *Student's Book*.

Exercise 8

This part of the lesson ends with students carrying out a mini-survey of three people. Students take turns to ask and answer questions about their abilities until the table is full.

ONE-TO-ONE With your one-to-one student, take turns to ask each other the questions in the table. For homework, ask your student to interview some other people in his/her workplace. Then for the next lesson, the student should prepare a summary of the results to present to you, as in **9**.

Exercise 9

Students might need to write their summaries of the results in the table before they read them aloud to the class. It also provides useful writing practice of the target structure.

Photocopiable worksheet
Download and photocopy *Unit 6 Language at work worksheet* from the teacher resources in the *Online practice*.

Practically speaking

Exercise 1

▶ 6.7 With false beginners, students could complete the list of days and then listen. Play the listening and students listen and check. It's useful to ask students to write the number of syllables they hear or ask them which day of the week has three syllables. Note that *Wednesday* causes problems for students as it appears to have three syllables on paper, but we only pronounce it with two. *Saturday* is the only day with three syllables.

Answer
See answers in audio script 6.7.

Exercise 2

Students ask each other the questions and say the day. You could also ask students to think of one more question for their partner using a verb they have learnt; for example, *What day do you play tennis?* or *What day do you have a meeting at work?*

EXTENSION In **2**, students probably answered with single words or short phrases, such as *Tuesday* or *three o'clock*. For complete answers, you will want them to add the prepositions *on* or *at*. Read the *Tip* together so students realize how we use the prepositions. For practice, you could ask them to repeat **2** with a new partner, and this time try to use a preposition before the day or time.

PRE-WORK LEARNERS For the first question, students can answer about when they go to college or university.

Exercise 3

After students have read the two notices, you could ask them if they have notices for free-time activities at work. Find out what they are for.

Answers
1 Monday at 5.00
2 Tuesday 12.00–1.00

Exercise 4

▶ 6.8 Allow students time to read the clocks. Some students might be able to guess the answers before listening. Make sure they write and say the words in full.

Answers
1 twelve
2 three
3 seven
4 eleven

Further practice
If students need more practice, go to *Practice file 6* on page 67 of the *Student's Book*.

Exercise 5

Students work in pairs again and ask questions about the time. They can also try to make their own questions asking about the time. For example, *What time do you have dinner?* or *What time do you play tennis?*

PRE-WORK LEARNERS For the first and third questions, students can answer about the times they start and finish at college or university.

Business communication

Exercise 1

▶ **6.9** It might be helpful to illustrate the meaning of the word *invitation* by asking different students questions, such as *Do you want to play tennis today?* or *Would you like to play tennis today?* Explain that this is an invitation. Then play the two conversations and match what the invitation is for.

Answers
Conversation 1: have dinner
Conversation 2: play tennis

Exercise 2

▶ **6.9** Students listen again to match the expressions. Alternatively, they could read the two halves and try to match them before listening again. Afterwards, they can check their answers by referring to the *Key expressions*.

Answers
1 b
2 d
3 a
4 i
5 e
6 c
7 f
8 h
9 g

EXTENSION For consolidation of these expressions, ask students to turn to page 78 and read the two conversations in audio script 6.9 aloud in pairs.

Exercise 3

▶ **6.10** Students could work in pairs to complete this activity, or you could do it orally as a class before listening to check.

Answers
1 b
2 a
3 b
4 b

Exercise 4

This provides controlled practice with the questions. Note that Student B (with the closed book) is allowed to use alternative expressions when answering, as long as they are correct.

PRONUNCIATION Note that some of the responses when accepting and declining require pronunciation that sounds sincere and polite. One way to help students with this is to draw attention to the stressed word in certain phrases. For example, write the following phrases on the board and say them with extra stress on the underlined word.

Yes, please. That'd be great! I'd love to.

I'm afraid I'm busy.

Students can listen and repeat or say them aloud, but don't underline the word on the board. Ask students to identify which word is stressed the most.

Further practice
If students need more practice, go to *Practice file 6* on page 66 of the *Student's Book*.

Exercise 5

Students study the flow chart and think about the kinds of expressions and phrases they will need. Then they practise the conversations. To extend the practice, students could swap partners and repeat the task. Make sure that everyone has the chance to invite the other person and to accept and decline.

Exercise 6

This is a free practice activity and students have the chance to invite each other to different events. As an alternative, ask all the students to stand and move around the room, inviting different people to different events.

Pay attention to the correct replies to questions and also the student's use of prepositions (*on* or *at*) when talking about days and times. Also make sure the expressions sound polite and sincere (see earlier note about pronunciation and sentence stress).

Photocopiable worksheet
Download and photocopy *Unit 6 Business communication worksheet* from the teacher resources in the *Online practice*.

Talking point

The context for this game is that students make conversation and small talk in between ordering a meal in a restaurant. You will need coins and counters for each group to move round the board. Demonstrate how students move the counters according to the coin flip and then model an answer for the square you land on.

As students move round and speak, avoid giving instant feedback, but take notes on any recurring errors. Then write these on the board and invite peer correction. You could follow up this feedback by asking students to return to the game in a later lesson, and simply ask and answer the questions and complete the tasks without counters as a revision exercise.

ONE-TO-ONE You can play the game with your student, with both of you flipping coins to move to different squares. Or you can just work through the squares, following the instructions. Make sure the student gets practice in both asking and answering questions.

Progress test

Download and photocopy *Unit 6 Progress test* and *Speaking test* from the teacher resources in the *Online practice*.

Unit content

By the end of this unit, students will be able to

- talk about office technology
- talk about what's in their office
- give instructions.

Context

Technology is part of everybody's working life, and this unit introduces students to the vocabulary they need to talk about different types of technology and the language they need to talk about using technology. This includes expressions for giving instructions to other people for using technology and dealing with it when it doesn't work.

In *Working with words*, students are introduced to the language for different technology through a reading text. It's the longest text that students will have read so far in *Business Result Starter* and will provide a sense of accomplishment. This is followed by three emails which include eight verbs that collocate with the technology nouns. *Language at work* presents possessive adjectives so that students can refer to their own technology, as well as other nouns.

In *Business communication*, students practise the *Key expressions* they need for asking for help with technology and for explaining how to use it. This will be helpful not only for students who work in engineering and technical areas, but also for employees in their everyday work.

In the *Talking point* at the end of the unit, students build on all the language from the unit by having to explain how different objects work.

Starting point

The first question revisits a topic the students looked at in *Unit 3*, but the aim is for them then to consider what type of technology they use in their workplace. The second question is a way to assess how much technology vocabulary the students already have. In addition, the names of some items of technology such as *iPad*, *iPhone*, and *tablet* are internationally used by speakers of other languages, so students may find they can answer the second question easily. Both questions then lead in to the text about the kind of technology that people use in different workplaces.

PRE-WORK LEARNERS For question 1, students can say where they study (at college or university, at home, in the library). For question 2, they can describe the technology at their place of study, or you could ask your students the question *What technology do you have today?*

Working with words

Exercise 1

▶ 7.1 You can either let students listen and read the text and then answer the questions, or you could ask them to read the text and answer without listening. Then after answering the questions, play the listening so that students can focus on how the words are said in the text.

Answers
1 Andrea
2 Mustafa
3 Julie

EXTRA ACTIVITY
For further reading practice, ask the students to answer these two questions for the three people in the text:

1 Where are they from? (Qatar, Brisbane in Australia, and the Netherlands.)
2 Where do they normally work? (In an office and on site, at home, and in an office.)

Exercise 2

Ask students to look at the pictures and say the names of any items they know. Then they find the words in the text and match them. Note that they will check their answers in **3**.

It may be helpful to draw attention to the *Tip* in the bottom left-hand corner of page 43 as it clarifies the abbreviations *PC* and *USB*.

Exercise 3

▶ 7.2 Students listen and check their answers. Then play the listening again and students repeat the words.

Answers
1 printer
2 USB stick
3 digital camera
4 webcam
5 headset
6 laptop
7 tablet
8 projector
9 smartphone
10 desktop computer

PRONUNCIATION Note that with all the two-syllable words in the list, the first syllable is stressed; for example, *lap*top, *smart*phone, *head*set, etc. The stress in the three-syllable word changes like this: *dig*ital, *cam*era, pro*jec*tor, com*pu*ter.

Exercise 4

Students can either tell their partner what items they have in **2** or, with small groups, students can tell the class.

PRE-WORK LEARNERS These students can talk about the technology they have at their college or university, or the technology they have at home.

Exercise 5

Students read three emails from the three people in **1**. They will need to consider the person's job and responsibilities in order to decide who wrote the email.

Answers
Email 1 Company logo, Julie
Email 2 Site report, Mustafa
Email 3 Presentation, Andrea

EXTENSION Students looked at emails in *Business communication* in *Unit 3*, so some of the language in these emails has already been presented. But students may have questions about the way they open with *Dear* or *Hi* and the way they end. It's also useful for them to notice the use of *Can* for requests and the *please* + imperative form in all three emails. Explain that we use them to ask for help and give instructions. Students might want to copy down any useful phrases for future use in their own emails. (See also suggestion for *Extra activity* after **7**.)

Exercise 6

Students analyse the use of the verbs in the emails and match them to the actions in the pictures. Note that some verbs match with the same item as in the email, but some change.

Answers
1 save
2 switch on
3 click
4 download
5 scan
6 print
7 enter
8 connect

Further practice

If students need more practice, go to *Practice file 7* on page 68 of the *Student's Book*.

Exercise 7

Students make basic sentences about what they do or don't do at work with different types of technology.

Monitor for correct combinations of verbs and nouns from the page.

PRE-WORK LEARNERS Ask students to talk about things they do / don't do at school / college.

EXTRA ACTIVITY
If your students often write emails, ask them to write a similar email to those in **5**. Write this situation on the board:

Write an email to your assistant:

You are out of the office. It is 3.00 p.m. Your presentation is at 3.30 p.m. Your presentation slides are on your PC. You need the presentation on a USB stick.

Students could write the email on their own, either in class or for homework, or they could work in pairs.

Photocopiable worksheet

Download and photocopy *Unit 7 Working with words worksheet* from the teacher resources in the *Online practice*.

Language at work

ALTERNATIVE If you think your students need extra help with the listening, play listening 7.3 once and ask: *How many people does Felipe meet?* (The answer is two.) This will give students an opportunity to get used to the whole listening before answering the more detailed questions in **1**.

Exercise 1

▶ **7.3** Give students time to read the five sentences and then play the listening. Ask students to compare answers with a partner before going through them as a class.

Answers
1 F (marketing assistant)
2 T
3 T
4 F (they are at a conference)
5 F (the PC and phone are on his desk, not the printer)

Exercise 2

▶ **7.3** Students could either listen and match, or they could read and try to match before listening to check.

Answers
1 c
2 f
3 g
4 a
5 b
6 d
7 e

Exercise 3

Students complete the table in the *Language point* with the highlighted possessive adjectives.

Answers

	Possessive adjectives
I	*my*
you	you
he	his
she	her
it	its
we	our
they	their

Grammar reference

If students need more information, go to *Grammar reference* on page 69 of the *Student's Book*.

Exercise 4

Students check their understanding and use of the possessive adjective.

Answers
2 their
3 His
4 Its
5 our
6 Her
7 Your

PRONUNCIATION It's important to check students can pronounce the possessive adjectives at this stage. Drill the list in the table in **3**. You could also drill them alongside the subject pronouns; for example, *I*, *my*, *you*, *your*, *he*, *his*, etc. It could also be useful to show students that the following words which they have learnt on the course so far have identical pronunciation (in most accents):

your = *you're*

its = *it's*

their = *they're* (or) *there*

EXTENSION There is a useful extension activity to use after these exercises:

For written practice, ask students to write seven similar sentences to those in **2**, but they write personal sentences with possessive adjectives about their own company, place of work, and the people they work with. (Pre-work learners can write about their college or university.)

Exercise 5

▶ **7.4** This exercise introduces students to the use of possessive *'s* after people's names and job titles. Students listen and read, and then answer.

Answer
The laptop is in the/their manager's office.

Exercise 6

▶ **7.4** Students listen again and circle the possessive *'s* in **5**.

Answers
Is it on Pierre(s)desk?
Is it in Remi and Ludo(s)office?
Is it in your manager(s)office?

Having circled the possessive *'s*, ask students to read the *Tip* with the explanation. In particular, note that with two names, the *'s* only comes after the second name.

EXTENSION For practice and consolidation, put students in pairs and ask them to read the A/B conversation in **5** aloud.

Further practice

If students need more practice, go to *Practice file 7* on page 69 of the *Student's Book*.

Exercise 7

The idea behind this activity is that each student has four different items of technology. They each assign one item to each of the people / places on their list in 1 (Student A) and in 2 (Student B). Then they take turns to ask and answer questions about who has the different objects. This requires use of the possessive 's.

Note that this activity requires students to make use of the prepositions of place *in* and *on*. Prepositions of place are not formally taught in *Business Result Starter* (see the *Elementary* level), but you may want to point out the simple difference between the phrases *on the desk* and *in the office*.

During the activity, make sure that students are clearly pronouncing the 's at the end of the names and that their pronunciation of the technology is correct.

Photocopiable worksheet

Download and photocopy *Unit 7 Language at work worksheet* from the teacher resources in the *Online practice*.

Practically speaking

This section introduces demonstrative pronouns, but students learn them as *this*, *that*, *these*, and *those*. It also provides a useful review and practice of the possessive adjectives from *Language at work*.

Exercise 1

Students match the sentences.

Answers
1 b
2 a
3 d
4 c

EXTENSION Before putting students in pairs for **2**, model the structures by pointing around the classroom at different objects and saying who they belong to. Elicit similar sentences from individual students.

Further practice

If students need more practice, go to *Practice file 7* on page 69 of the *Student's Book*.

Exercise 2

Students work in pairs and talk about their own objects. If you want them to refer to a wider range of objects than simply those in their bags or in the classroom, you could bring some real objects in or provide pictures of objects for students to use.

PRONUNCIATION In *Language at work* and *Practically speaking*, students have been working on a number of new words that either have identical vowel sounds or sounds which are slightly different. A simple awareness-raising activity is to write this set of words randomly around the board and ask students to group the words according to vowel sounds. The list contains words from this unit and a few from previous units:

this those she there three that six its these he his I at keys their my we five oh

Answers
this, six, his, its /ɪ/
those, oh /əʊ/
these, she, three, he, we, keys /iː/
there, their /eə/
that, at /æ/
I, my, five /aɪ/

Business communication

Exercise 1

Many of your students may be very familiar with video conferencing and use it a lot, but some may not be familiar with it. If so, ask students to look at the picture and begin by asking them why we use video conference equipment. If you have students who use it, ask them to explain what kind of meeting they have on it and why this technology is useful in their work. They can describe their uses with the present simple and *can* for ability, for example *I have meetings with colleagues* or *I can speak to clients in other countries*. Next, students say what technology you need. They can re-use vocabulary taught in *Working with words*.

Possible answers
(depending on the type of video conference equipment)
screen, webcam, PC, laptop or tablet, Internet, keyboard, microphone, headset

Exercise 2

▶ **7.5** Students read the scenario and then listen for the names of any technology.

Answers
headset and microphone

Exercise 3

▶ **7.5** Students listen again to match the questions and responses.

Answers
1 g
2 d
3 a
4 c
5 f
6 b
7 e

EXTENSION Before moving on to **4**, students could work in pairs and turn to audio script 7.5 on page 79. They read the conversation aloud to build confidence with the new expressions.

Exercise 4

To recreate the conversation between Ryan and Amanda, students need to make use of the pictures and the language in **3**. They could try it a couple of times, and then cover the language in **3** so that they only refer to the pictures and try to recreate the conversation from memory, using the pictures.

Further practice
If students need more practice, go to *Practice file 7* on page 68 of the *Student's Book*.

Exercise 5

Students turn to the pages indicated and study the pictures and verb prompts for giving instructions for scanning documents on a new printer (Student A) and downloading photographs from a digital camera to a laptop (Student B). When they are ready to speak, they present the process to their partner. The partner should also look at the pictures

and say appropriate expressions from the *Key expressions*, such as *I don't know how to use …* or *How does it work?*

Give feedback on both how well students can ask for help with technology and the way in which they give instructions; in particular, make sure they are using the sequencers (*First, Next, Then*) to structure the information. This is a useful skill that they can transfer into all their future presentation work.

EXTENSION Ask your student or students to think of an important item of technology in their workplace, or perhaps they could explain a short process in their work. Then they prepare a short presentation for the next lesson, ideally with visual aids to help the demonstration.

Photocopiable worksheet
Download and photocopy *Unit 7 Business communication worksheet* from the teacher resources in the *Online practice*.

Talking point

The main aim of the game is for students to guess which piece of technology is being described. Put students into groups of four and then into two teams in each group. Ideally, make sure you have stronger and weaker students working together in each pair.

Before a team describes its choice, they might need a few minutes to prepare. One option is to ask both teams to prepare their descriptions at the same time and then take turns to describe it.

Some of the terms may be new to them in English, but the students should be aware of the technology in their own language. If this is the case, use this as an opportunity to teach the new items (for example, *wireless*, *smartwatch*, *Bluetooth*, *the Cloud*).

Answers
1 printer
2 USB stick
3 projector
4 laptop
5 games console
6 social media (Twitter)
7 wireless (Bluetooth) speaker
8 Bluetooth
9 Wi-fi
10 microphone
11 webcam
12 smartphone
13 remote control
14 the Cloud
15 smartwatch
16 headphones

EXTRA ACTIVITY

To practise any new vocabulary, put students into pairs or teams to see how many of items 1–16 they can remember. This could be done as a game in which Student/Team A challenges Student/Team B to identify an item (for example, *What is square 14?*)

ONE-TO-ONE You can take turns with the student to describe and guess.

Progress test

Download and photocopy *Unit 7 Progress test* and *Speaking test* from the teacher resources in the *Online practice*.

8 Travel

Context

Despite the growing number of ways that business people can communicate with clients and colleagues without having to travel (e.g. via video conferencing), the number of people taking business trips is greater than ever. So, many business English students need the language for travel and for making necessary arrangements when on the move. In this unit, students begin by learning key vocabulary for talking about transport. They also practise the words, phrases, and questions they'll need for situations such as taking a taxi or catching a flight.

Having learnt how to use the present simple in previous units, students are also introduced to talking about the past with *was / were* in *Language at work*. This is presented in the context of reporting on how a business trip is going, with a traveller giving updates on various meetings. This leads into students talking about months and dates, which builds on the work done on saying days and times in *Unit 6*.

In *Business communication*, students practise the key expressions they need for arranging a meeting both by email and on the phone.

The *Talking point* that follows extends this into a series of staged activities involving filling in a calendar and arranging a date. Finally, if you have followed the units in order and this is the final unit of your course, there is an additional *Revision game* which you can download from the teacher resources in the *Online practice* to help students review all the language they have covered in *Business Result Starter*.

Starting point

The first question revises the language for saying times from *Practically speaking* in *Unit 6* and leads into the topic of commuting and travelling for your job. Use the opportunity to check students can remember how to say times and talk about parts of their daily routines.

Note the use of the verb *take* to describe the length of time a journey takes. You might need to clarify this use of *take* and point out that we use this verb in different ways in English. (Note that in the listening in *Working with words* students will hear it used again to refer to taking transport; it is also shown in a *Tip* box.)

Having discussed the topic of travelling to work and travelling for work, students should compare the use of *go* and *travel*, when talking about everyday travel and travel for long journeys. Ask students to read the *Tip* and then write and say two similar sentences with *go* and *travel* about their own working or student life.

PRE-WORK LEARNERS   Adapt the *Starting point* questions so that these students talk about what time they leave for and arrive at their place of study. For question 2, ask them: *Do you travel on holiday?* and *Where do you travel on holiday?*

Working with words

Exercise 1

Students study the pie chart and answer the three questions.

Answers
1 24%
2 7%
3 48%

EXTENSION Students can work in pairs and write two more questions starting with the words *What percentage of people …?* They complete the question with transport words from the pie chart; for example, *What percentage of people go to work by motorcycle?* Then they work with another pair and ask and answer their questions.

Exercise 2

▶ **8.1** Students practise the pronunciation of the five transport words.

Exercise 3

Draw students' attention to the question in the chart about Japan in **1**: *How do people go to work in Japan?* Students haven't used questions starting with *How* before, so make sure they realize that in this context it is asking about the type of transport.

Next, students stand up and move around interviewing people in the class and getting results on how they travel to work. If you are teaching a very large class, you might need to put students into smaller groups so that they only interview seven or eight people each.

ONE-TO-ONE Ask the student to complete the table by asking you the question and ticking your answer.

Exercise 4

Students compare their results in pairs and draw a pie chart to reflect the results. If they have a few differences in their answers, they can take an average. Ideally students should draw their pie charts on large pieces of paper so that everyone can see the results in their presentations.

PRE-WORK LEARNERS If you teach a pre-work class, this activity is a useful opportunity to set some project work. Students could research how people travel to work in their own country by looking for information online. Alternatively, they could continue interviewing other students outside class about how they travel to college, and then report back their findings with pie charts at the next lesson.

ONE-TO-ONE Introduce the question in the third person and ask about other people your student works with; for example, *How does your boss go to work? How does your colleague go to work?*, etc.

Exercise 5

▶ **8.2** Students listen to two conversations with a person going on a business trip and tick the type of transport he is taking.

Answers
Conversation 1: taxi
Conversation 2: plane

Exercise 6

The conversations make reference to different places and items on a business trip. To pre-teach these, students match the words to the pictures.

Answers
a receipt
b terminal
c passport
d e-ticket
e boarding gate
f bag

Exercise 7

Students complete the questions and sentences from the listening which contain words from **6** and eight verbs. If necessary, play the listening so students can fill in the questions and sentences while they listen. Note that the answers are given as part of **8**.

Exercise 8

▶ **8.2** Students listen and check.

When looking at the answer in 1 with *take*, refer students to the *Tip* and the explanation of *take* to mean travel by a type of transport.

Answers
1 take
2 want
3 want
4 have
5 check in
6 leave
7 go
8 arrive

EXTENSION For consolidation of the language (and preparation for the next activity), students could turn to audio script 8.2 on page 79 and read it aloud in pairs.

Further practice

If students need more practice, go to *Practice file 8* on page 70 of the *Student's Book*.

Exercise 9

This is a role-play task with prompts provided for the pairs of students. Before speaking, students could read the role-plays and match suitable expressions from **7** and think about answers for each prompt. Then they can practise each conversation and swap roles and repeat. With stronger classes, suggest students change the names of the destinations and prices to vary the conversations.

Give feedback on the correct use of the vocabulary and expressions from this page. In particular, monitor closely for correct verb + noun collocates.

Photocopiable worksheet

Download and photocopy *Unit 8 Working with words worksheet* from the teacher resources in the *Online practice*.

Language at work

Exercise 1

▶ **8.3** Ask students to read the situation and check understanding by asking *Where is Donald Jones?* (Answer: in his office) and *Who does he work with?* (Answer: Alice). Ask them to look at the list of places in 1–3 and say which region of the world they are in (Answer: the Middle East). Then play the listening and students match 1–4 to a–d.

Answers
1 b
2 d
3 a
4 c

Exercise 2

▶ **8.3** Explain that *was* and *were* are the past forms of the verb *to be*. Give a couple of examples such as *I was on holiday yesterday* and *You were at work yesterday*. Then students listen and underline the correct verb forms.

Answers
1 was
2 was
3 were
4 wasn't
5 were
6 weren't
7 Were
8 wasn't

Exercise 3

Students check their understanding of the past simple of the verb *to be* by completing the three sentences in the *Language point*.

Answers
We use *am / is / are* for the verb *be* in the present.
We use *was / were* for the verb *be* in the past.
We use *wasn't / weren't* for the past of the verb *be* in the negative.

Grammar reference

If students need more information, go to *Grammar reference* on page 71 of the *Student's Book*.

EXTENSION You could also clarify the use of *was / were* by drawing this language summary table on the board and asking students to copy and complete it with *was*, *were*, *wasn't*, or *weren't*.

Positive	Negative	Questions	Short answers
I / He / She /It ¹_____ in Oman.	I / He / She / It ³_____ on holiday.	⁵_____ he / she / it in Muscat?	Yes, I / he / she / it ⁷_____.
You / We / They ²_____ in Oman.	You / We / They ⁴_____ on holiday.	⁶_____ you / we / they at work?	No, you / we / they ⁸_____.

Afterwards, students could turn to the *Grammar reference* on page 71 and check their answers.

Answers
1 was
2 were
3 wasn't
4 weren't
5 Was
6 Were
7 was
8 weren't

Exercise 4

▶ **8.4** Students check their use of the correct form by completing the rest of the conversation.

After students listen and check, they could listen again and repeat sentences to practise the correct pronunciation of the verb forms.

Answers
1 was
2 were
3 wasn't
4 were
5 was
6 weren't

Exercise 5

Students work together to make sentences with *was* and *were* about the story of Donald and Alice's business trip.

Possible answer
They were in Paris last Monday and Tuesday. On Wednesday, Donald was in a meeting, but Alice wasn't. Then they were in a restaurant. They were in Milan at a trade fair on Thursday and Friday.

EXTENSION Model the question form needed by asking students about the pictures. For example:

Where were they last Monday and Tuesday?

Where was Donald on Wednesday? Where was Alice?

Where were they on Thursday and Friday?

You could also ask *Yes / No* questions to elicit short answers. For example:

Were they in Paris on Monday? Yes, they were.

Was Alice in a meeting on Wednesday? No, she wasn't.

After you have demonstrated use of the question forms, put students in pairs and ask them to ask each other similar questions about the pictures.

Exercise 6

Students ask and answer questions about their own past. After they have interviewed one partner, they can swap and interview someone else. Input any necessary words for their answers, such as names of places.

Further practice

If students need more practice, go to *Practice file 8* on page 71 of the *Student's Book*.

Exercise 7

Students turn to the pages indicated with fictional diaries and a list of places they were in on different days. Student A begins by studying a gapped version of Student B's diary and asking questions with *were* to find out the days and places missing from the diary. Then they swap roles, with Student B asking questions about Student A's diary.

Concentrate on whether students are forming *was / were* questions correctly and give on-the-spot help to any students who need reminding of the correct form.

Photocopiable worksheet

Download and photocopy *Unit 8 Language at work worksheet* from the teacher resources in the *Online practice*.

Practically speaking

Exercise 1

▶ **8.5** As well as listening and repeating the months, students could underline the stressed syllable in each month.

Answers

<u>Ja</u>nuary <u>Fe</u>bruary March <u>A</u>pril May June July Au<u>gust</u> Sep<u>tem</u>ber Oc<u>to</u>ber No<u>vem</u>ber De<u>cem</u>ber

Exercise 2

▶ **8.6** Students listen to two people talking about a schedule of events in the past and in the future and concentrate on only listening for the four months they mention.

Answers

June, August, September, November

Exercise 3

▶ **8.6** Now they study the actual schedule discussed in the conversation and mark the calendar with the relevant dates.

Answers

1st June – last trip to Turin
3rd to 14th August – next trip
11th September – factory visit
27th to 30th November – sales conference

Exercise 4

▶ **8.7** Students practise saying the dates from the schedule in **3**. As a follow-up, drill the endings of the dates and check everyone can say the endings *-st*, *-rd*, *-th*.

Further practice

If students need more practice, go to *Practice file 8* on page 71 of the *Student's Book*.

Exercise 5

Students ask and answer the questions with real dates.

Ask students to read the *Tip*, and for practice they could write the dates in **5** in the three different ways. If any of your students have contact with people in North America, point out that dates in American English have the month first and the day second; e.g. *the eighteenth of March = 3/18*.

Business communication

Exercise 1

Students read the email and check their understanding of the key information. You could also ask the students how many people Simon is sending the email to (Answer: two people, called Ines and Frieda).

Answers
1 on Tuesday 30th August
2 at 11 a.m.
3 a sales trip in September

Exercise 2

The replies to Simon's email in **1** are from Ines and Frieda.

Answers
1 Frieda can go to the meeting.
2 Ines can't go because she's visiting a factory.

Exercise 3

▶ **8.8** As a result of the emails, Simon calls Ines to arrange a meeting.

Answer
on Thursday 1st September at 10 a.m.

Exercise 4

▶ **8.8** As an alternative to listening and writing, students could try to complete the conversation with the phrases before listening. They could also use the list in the *Key expressions* to check their answers.

Answers
1 Can we arrange
2 Are you free
3 I'm busy
4 How about
5 I'm free
6 What time
7 Is, OK

Exercise 5

▶ **8.9** Students match more useful expressions for arranging to meet and then listen to check.

Answers
1 c
2 a
3 d
4 f
5 b
6 e

Further practice

If students need more practice, go to *Practice file 8* on page 70 of the *Student's Book*.

Exercise 6

Students turn to the pages indicated and role-play a phone conversation to arrange a meeting. Afterwards, they can swap roles and repeat the phone call.

The main part of this task is to ensure that students understand the reason for the meeting and that they manage to arrange a meeting, so check that students manage to do this. Then focus on the correct use of expressions. Students should also be making use of dates, times, and months, and these will need to be pronounced well, so drill words and sounds that continue to cause difficulty and confusion.

EXTENSION Students can create their own role-plays by writing down a reason to meet with a time and date and then call another student to arrange a meeting. (Note also that students will get more practice with the language for arranging meetings in the *Talking point* on page 53 of the *Student's Book*.)

Photocopiable worksheet

Download and photocopy *Unit 8 Business communication worksheet* from the teacher resources in the *Online practice*.

Talking point

The aim of this activity is to arrange a meeting between four people. However, before students speak to each other, they have to read and listen to various pieces of information which will affect when they can meet. Put students into groups of four and then divide them into pairs A and B. Pair B needs to turn to page 75.

Exercise 1

Both pairs read their own sets of information. After they have filled in the calendar, try to check that each pair has completed the calendars correctly.

> **Answers**
> Pair A
> 18–23 April: Frankfurt (Sales conference 20–22 April)
> 8–11 May: Sales trip to Hungary
> Pair B
> 15–20 April: Bangkok (Sales conference 17–18 April)
> 1–5 May: Sales trip to Hungary

ONE-TO-ONE Your student can take the part of Pair A while you take the part of Pair B.

Exercise 2

▶ **8.10** Having filled in the calendars, all students listen to a voicemail and add the information to their calendars.

> **Answer**
> Meeting at head office on 29th April at 9 a.m.

Exercise 3

Finally, the four students arrange to meet as if they are having a teleconference. You could sit them back to back to simulate a teleconference. They arrange the meeting based on the free dates and times they have left in their calendars. Afterwards, ask all the groups to tell the class which time and date they agreed upon.

Progress test

Download and photocopy *Unit 8 Progress test* and *Speaking test* from the teacher resources in the *Online practice*.

The revision game

Download and print out *The revision game* from the teacher resources in the *Online practice*.

Having completed all eight units in *Business Result Starter*, this game provides a natural ending to the course and a chance to review all the language taught.

Students work in pairs and can each start on any square around the edges of the board. If they choose a conversation square, they start a conversation with their partner similar to many of the role-play activities that they have done in the book. On the instruction square, they read and complete the task, many of which are oriented to remembering key vocabulary, grammar, or expressions. The question square means they have to answer the question or questions on the square. Once they have completed the task on the square, they tick it. Then they move on to another square. Students can move horizontally, vertically, or diagonally in order to complete five squares.

Once a pair finishes the game, they can start again or simply choose different squares and complete the tasks. If they have problems remembering language they need, tell students to look back through the book and find the relevant pages to help them. As you listen to the students, make a note of any language areas that are causing difficulty and will need reviewing again at a later stage.

Viewpoint 2

Preview

The topic of this *Viewpoint* is *Describing businesses*. It recycles vocabulary from all eight units of the book and also introduces some new terms. In this *Viewpoint*, students watch two videos about two very different types of business. One is about the large charity organization Oxfam and its chain of high street shops. The second is about a self-employed consultant operating out of his own home. With both videos, students need to listen carefully and answer questions or complete sentences. At the end, students apply the vocabulary to making notes about their own business or organization and then writing a short description of their company.

Exercise 1

This exercise introduces and pre-teaches key vocabulary that students will need to understand the videos. Most words appear in the previous units, but you may need to remind students or help them with new words such as *charity*. You could do the first word (*international*) in sentence 1 together as a class and then let students work on their own or in pairs to match the rest.

Answers

a builds
b international
c self-employed
d order
e charity
f exports
g face-to-face
h run

PRONUNCIATION Before continuing, you will need to help students say all the words correctly in **1**. Drill the words and focus on any causing difficulty – you could focus on the stress in longer words such as *inter<u>na</u>tional*, *self-em<u>ployed</u>*, *<u>cha</u>rity*. You could also read all six sentences out loud and then, working in pairs, students could read the sentences to their partner so that they feel confident using the words in context.

Exercise 2

Students can choose any of the words that describe their own business or organization and tell their partner.

PRE-WORK LEARNERS Ask students to think of a company they know to answer the question in **2**.

EXTENSION Ask students to write short sentences about their business (or a company they know for pre-work learners) using the words chosen.

Exercise 3

▶ 01 Tell the students that Oxfam is a very large charity in the UK. Point out the photo showing the Oxfam logo and shop at the bottom of the page and ask if they know the name *Oxfam* in their country. Then allow time for students

to read the five topics, and clarify any vocabulary such as *volunteers* (given in the *Glossary*).

Then play the video and ask students to number the topics in the order they see them in the video.

Answers

4 small businesses and farmers
2 employees and volunteers in other countries
1 the Oxfam head office
3 children in schools
5 Oxfam shops

If necessary, when checking the answers play the video again and pause it at different stages to clarify which topic is on the screen.

VIDEO SCRIPT

Oxfam is a large international charity. The head office is in Oxford in the UK. Seven hundred people work here. Oxfam also has employees and volunteers all over the world. They provide food and medicine. They build wells for clean water. They build schools and help children to get an education. They also work with small businesses. With help from Oxfam, many farmers sell their products in local markets, and some people export products to other countries.

Many people give money to Oxfam every month because Oxfam needs money for its work. Oxfam also has 700 shops in the UK. People give old books and clothes to the shops, and then they sell them. You can even order clothes from Oxfam shops online. All the money from the shops helps Oxfam with its good work.

Exercise 4

▶ 01 Allow time for students to read the eight questions. All the vocabulary in questions 1–8 should be familiar to them, but it's worth checking before students watch the video. They could even try and answer any questions they think they already know before watching again. Then play the video.

Answers

1 700
2 food and medicine
3 for clean water
4 builds schools for them to get an education
5 in local markets, and as exports
6 money
7 old books and clothes
8 from Oxfam shops and online

Exercise 5

Put students into small groups and give them five minutes to discuss the questions about charities. You may need to clarify the difference between *national* and *international*. One person in the group could take notes and feed back the answers at the end.

Exercise 6

▶ **02** Students should read sentences 1–5 and try to predict the correct answers before watching. Make sure they realize that in one sentence, both answers are correct.

Answers
1. is self-employed
2. the UK
3. online and face-to-face (both answers correct)
4. website
5. their offices

VIDEO SCRIPT

This is Mike Phips. He's a self-employed trainer.
I run training courses in management and communication. My clients are all over the UK. Some courses are online webinars, and some are face-to-face in a company.
Mike sells a lot of his services online. Clients can buy training courses from his website. Clients download documents for online courses.
Mike uses a webcam to run training sessions from his office.
For face-to-face courses, Mike visits companies and organizations and works with employees in their offices.

Exercise 7

Students complete the sentences with the pairs of words and compare their answers with a partner. Note that the answers are given as part of **8**.

Exercise 8

▶ **02** Play the video again for students to check their answers in **7**.

Answers
1. run + courses
2. sells + services
3. buy + courses
4. visits + organizations
5. works + employees

PRONUNCIATION Before moving onto the final section, it is a good moment to review some of the key vocabulary from this *Viewpoint* and check students are confident with the pronunciation. Write the following words and word stress patterns on the board. Students have to match the words to the correct stress pattern. Then drill the words afterwards, eliciting their meanings.

employed   exports   charity   volunteer   employee communication   organization   courses   services management   clients   customers

●● · ●● · ●●· · ●●● · ●●●●●

Answers
●●   courses, clients
●●   employed, exports
●●··   charity, services, management, customers
●●●   volunteer
●●●●●   organization, communication

Exercise 9

Students can work on their own, or if the students work for the same company, they could work in pairs or small groups. The activity allows students to use vocabulary from the two videos and also revises language from all eight units.

PRE-WORK LEARNERS Ask students to think of a company they know well, or ask them to research the company and write information about it in the table. They could carry out the research online or in class, or you could set the research task for homework.

Exercise 10

Students imagine they are going to make an informational video about their own company and write the narrative description to go with it using their notes from **9**. There are different approaches to this task. Students could write it quite impersonally like a documentary, similar to the Oxfam video. Or, students could describe their company from a more personal perspective, perhaps including interviews similar to the video about Mike Phips.

PRE-WORK LEARNERS Students use the notes they made in **9** about a company they know well to do this exercise.

Exercise 11

Students take turns to read their descriptions to each other. Alternatively, students could read their descriptions in small groups.

Further video ideas

You can find a list of suggested ideas for how to use video in the class in the teacher resources in the *Online practice*.

Practice file answer key

Unit 1

Working with words

Exercise 1
2 my name **3** Hi **4** I'm

Exercise 2
1 b **2** a

Exercise 3
1 technician   **4** manager
2 finance   **5** engineer
3 assistant   **6** representative

Exercise 4
3 an **4** a **5** a **6** an **7** an **8** a

Exercise 5
1 an engineer   **3** a sales representative
2 an IT technician   **4** a finance director

Business communication

Exercise 1
1 a 3 **b** 1 **c** 2
2 a 1 **b** 3 **c** 2
3 a 3 **b** 2 **c** 1

Exercise 2
1 Good   **5** this is
2 I'm   **6** too
3 surname   **7** See you
4 Are   **8** meeting

Practically speaking
1 K **2** E/T **3** T/E **4** N/X **5** X/N **6** Y **7** U

Language at work

Exercise 1
1 'm **2** are **3** 'm **4** are

Exercise 2
1 're **2** 'm not **3** 'm **4** 're not

Exercise 3
1 am **2** Are **3** 'm not

Exercise 4
1 Are **2** am **3** 'm not

Exercise 5
1 a **2** b **3** b **4** a **5** b **6** a

Unit 2

Working with words

Exercise 1
1 Samsung   **3** company
2 South Korea   **4** office

Exercise 2
1 Brazil   **5** South Korea
2 Saudi Arabia   **6** China
3 Japan   **7** Spain
4 Germany   **8** Kuwait

Exercise 3
1 Taro Nakamura, Japan, Honda, Tokyo
2 Jenny Thomas, the USA, Nike, Oregon
3 Robert Bosisio, Spain, Inditex, Arteixo

Exercise 4
1 Where are you from?
2 Where is your head office?
3 What is your company?

Exercise 5
a 3 **b** 2 **c** 1

Business communication

Exercise 1
1 a 3 **b** 2 **c** 4 **d** 1
2 a 3 **b** 1 **c** 4 **d** 2

Exercise 2
1 speaking   **5** It's
2 there   **6** in the office
3 One moment   **7** out
4 that

Exercise 3
1 speak   **3** One
2 of course   **4** OK, thanks

Practically speaking
1 c **2** d **3** a **4** b

Language at work

Exercise 1
1 isn't   **4** 's
2 's   **5** 's
3 isn't   **6** isn't

Exercise 2
1 b **2** c **3** a

Exercise 3
1 b **2** a **3** b **4** b **5** a **6** b **7** b **8** a

Exercise 4
1 Is **2** is **3** isn't **4** 's **5** Is **6** isn't **7** 's **8** isn't **9** 's
10 Is **11** isn't **12** 's

Unit 3

Working with words

Exercise 1

⁵R	E	²C	E	P	T	I	O	N	
E	⁴C	A	R	P	A	R	K	⁶O	
C	A	F	Z	A	³F	L	T	F	
D	Y	E	O	T	A	O	A	F	
E	M	T	T	U	C	D	X	I	
H	N	E	O	F	T	T	O	C	
¹W	A	R	E	H	O	U	S	E	
O	R	I	A	W	R	E	C	E	
N	F	A	C	T	Y	W	H	I	

Exercise 2
1 c 2 a 3 b

Exercise 3
2 an old factory
3 a good cafeteria
4 a big car park
5 a small warehouse

Business communication

Exercise 1
1 Thanks   3 Please
2 Here   4 All

Exercise 2
1 Dear   3 Can you
2 I'm writing   4 Best

Exercise 3
1 c 2 a 3 e 4 b 5 d

Exercise 4
2 Thank you   4 Please find
3 Can you   5 wishes (or regards)

Practically speaking
1 a 2 c 3 b

Language at work

Exercise 1
1 're / are   5 Are
2 aren't   6 aren't
3 're / are   7 Are
4 aren't   8 are

Exercise 2
1 **I'm** are a manager.
2 **Are** is you an IT technician?
3 Yes, he **is** are.
4 No, they **aren't** isn't.

Exercise 3
1 d 2 c 3 f 4 a 5 b 6 e

Exercise 4
1 What's   4 Where are
2 Where are   5 Who's
3 What's

Unit 4

Working with words

Exercise 1
1 sell   4 manage
2 meet   5 have
3 work   6 live

Exercise 2
1 live   4 have
2 work   5 manage
3 sell   6 meet

Exercise 3
1 d 2 f 3 a 4 c 5 e 6 b

Exercise 4
1 companies   5 departments
2 customers   6 countries
3 people   7 employees
4 offices   8 factories

Business communication

Exercise 1
1 R 2 C 3 C 4 R 5 R 6 R

Exercise 2
Part 1
a 2 b 5 c 1 d 3 e 4 f 6
Part 2
g 1 h 3 i 7 j 2 k 6 l 4 m 5

Exercise 3
1 Can I take a message?
2
A I'm calling about
B Can you repeat that?
3
A Please call me back as soon as possible.
B So that's
B I'll give Claudia your message.

Practically speaking
1 are   4 are
2 's   5 's
3 's   6 are

Language at work

Exercise 1
1 I work   5 I work
2 don't live   6 I manage
3 I live   7 They don't sell
4 We have   8 They meet

Exercise 2
2 Do you work in Finance? No, we don't.
3 Do they have factories in Germany? Yes, they do.
4 Do they manage people? No, they don't.

Exercise 3
1 c 2 e 3 f 4 a 5 b 6 d

Exercise 4
1 What do you do?
2 Who do you work for?
3 Where do they live?
4 Who do you work for?
5 What do they do?

Unit 5

Working with words

Exercise 1
1 c **2** d **3** b **4** e **5** a

Exercise 2
1 make
2 sell
3 have
4 order
5 design
6 buy
7 build

Exercise 3
1 American
2 Brazil
3 Chinese
4 England
5 Italian
6 India
7 Japanese
8 Mexico

Business communication

Exercise 1
1 Can I help you?
2 Do you have the item number?
3 How many would you like?
4 What's the price?
5 Does that include delivery?
6 Can you confirm my order by email?

Exercise 2
a 4 **b** 5 **c** 3 **d** 6 **e** 1 **f** 2

Exercise 3
1 help
2 order
3 have
4 like
5 want
6 include
7 confirm
8 email

Practically speaking
1 60,000,000
2 53,000
3 365
4 11

Language at work

Exercise 1
1 exports
2 sells
3 builds
4 doesn't import
5 doesn't buy
6 doesn't build
7 has

Exercise 2
1 sells
2 sell
3 designs
4 deliver
5 doesn't have
6 don't make

Exercise 3
1 **A** <u>Does</u> Toyota <u>make</u> cars?
  B Yes, it <u>does</u>.
2 **A** <u>Does</u> Apple <u>deliver</u> food?
  B No, it <u>doesn't</u>.
3 **A** <u>Does</u> Walmart <u>sell</u> food and clothes?
  B Yes, it <u>does</u>.

Exercise 4
1 Do
2 does
3 does
4 Do
5 do
6 Does

Unit 6

Working with words

Exercise 1
1 ice cream
2 steak and fries
3 mineral water
4 chocolate cake
5 cheese sandwich
6 tea
7 salad
8 orange juice

Exercise 2
1 can I help you
2 would you like
3 I'd like
4 can I have
5 I'd like
6 that's
7 That's

Exercise 3
1 What food do you like?
2 I like steak and fries.
3 I don't like Mexican food.
4 I don't like rice, but I like pasta. / I like rice, but I don't like pasta.
5 Do you like Japanese food?
6 I like Chinese food.

Business communication

Exercise 1
1 a 5 **b** 3 **c** 1 **d** 6 **e** 4 **f** 2
2 a 3 **b** 5 **c** 2 **d** 4 **e** 1

Exercise 2
1 Would you like to have dinner on Tuesday?
2 What time can you meet?
3 Do you want to play tennis on Wednesday?
4 Is two thirty OK?
5 What day can you play?

Exercise 3
a 4 **b** 5 **c** 1 **d** 2 **e** 3

Practically speaking

Exercise 1
Monday, Tuesday, Wednesday, Thursday, Friday, Saturday, Sunday

Exercise 2
1 d **2** c **3** e **4** a **5** b

Language at work

Exercise 1
2 She can't cook.
3 They can't run a marathon.
4 I can play a musical instrument.
5 He can play tennis.

Exercise 2
2 Can he cook Indian food?
  No, he can't.
3 Can she play the guitar?
  No, she can't.
4 Can she speak other languages?
  Yes, she can.

Exercise 3

1 can't **2** Can he **3** can't **4** Can you **5** can't

Exercise 4

1 What sports can you play?
2 What languages can she speak?
3 What types of food can Simon cook?
4 What musical instrument can they play?

Exercise 5

a 3 **b** 4 **c** 2 **d** 1

Unit 7

Working with words

Exercise 1

1 laptop **4** projector
2 webcam **5** printer
3 headset

Exercise 2

1 webcam **3** USB stick
2 smartphone **4** computer

Exercise 3

1 Click **4** save
2 enter **5** connect
3 Download **6** Print

Business communication

Exercise 1

a What **d** Is
b How **e** Does
c Do **f** Where

Exercise 2

1 a **2** b **3** d **4** f **5** e **6** c

Exercise 3

1 First **2** Then **3** Next **4** need

Exercise 4

1 b **2** a **3** b **4** a **5** b

Practically speaking

1 That **2** These **3** Those **4** This

Language at work

Exercise 1

1 my **2** your **3** our **4** his **5** her **6** their **7** its

Exercise 2

1 your **2** My **3** My **4** It's **5** Her **6** He's **7** Our **8** They

Exercise 3

1 Is this Mike's headset?
2 Juliette and Medhat's office is here.
3 Rosa's computer is on, so she's here.
4 Where is Remi, Sultan, and Ricardo's meeting today?

Exercise 4

1 His name is Mike.
2 Is this my new mobile?
3 Hello. This is Nigel's voicemail.
4 The printer is old and it's slow.
5 Their office is there and our office is here.

Unit 8

Working with words

Exercise 1

1 d **2** e **3** b **4** f **5** a **6** g **7** c

Exercise 2

1 terminal **5** passport
2 receipt **6** boarding gate
3 e-ticket **7** flight
4 bag

Exercise 3

1 have **5** arrive
2 go **6** want
3 want **7** leaves
4 take **8** check in

Business communication

Exercise 1

1 I'd like to arrange
2 Can we meet on
3 I can't meet
4 we arrange a new date and time
5 is fine for me

Exercise 2

1 I'd like to arrange a meeting.
2 I'm sorry, I can't meet at 2 p.m.
3 Are you free on Monday at 3.30 p.m.? / Are you free at 3.30 p.m. on Monday?
4 13th April is fine for me.

Exercise 3

a 2 **b** 6 **c** 1 **d** 5 **e** 3 **f** 4

Practically speaking

1 e **2** d **3** b **4** a **5** c

Language at work

Exercise 1

1 was **4** wasn't
2 wasn't **5** weren't
3 were **6** was

Exercise 2

2 Were they busy yesterday?
   No, they weren't.
3 Was he there last week?
   No, he wasn't.
4 Was the city quiet last night?
   Yes, it was.

Exercise 3

1 Were **2** wasn't **3** was **4** was **5** was **6** weren't
7 Were **8** wasn't **9** was

Exercise 4

1 Where were you last Monday?
2 When were they in Santiago?
3 How long was she in Dubai?
4 How was your business trip?

Exercise 5

a 4 **b** 1 **c** 3 **d** 2